The Wrestling

Simon Garfield

faber and faber

First published in 1996
by Faber and Faber Limited
3 Queen Square London WC1N 3AU
This new paperback edition first published in 2007

Typeset by Faber and Faber Limited
Printed in England by CPI Group (UK) Ltd, Croydon, CRO 4YY

A CIP record for this book
is available from the British Library

ISBN 978-0-571-23676-3

10 9 8 7 6 5 4 3

Contents

The Wrestling

Featuring:

Bill Abbey, a promoter

Bobby Barnes, a heel

Roland Barthes, a semiologist

Big Daddy, a blue-eye

Big Jim Harris the Mississippi
Mauler, a heel

Peter Blake, an artist, a fan

Dave Soulman Bond, a heel

Don Branch, a blue-eye

Wayne Bridges, a blue-eye

Robbie Brookside, a blue-eye

Frank Casey, a blue-eye,
a maker of bedroom furniture

CB Cochran, a promoter

Brian Crabtree, an MC

Max Crabtree, a promoter

Dickie Davies, a broadcaster

Doc Dean, a blue-eye

Alan Dennison, a strongman

Jimmy Savile:
I was very very bad

Brian Dixon, a promoter

Joe D'Orazio, a referee

Ian Dury, a singer, a painter

Greg Dyke, a television
executive

Brian Howard Finkel,
an American expert

Simon Garfield, a narrator

Giant Haystacks, a heel

Brian Glover, a heel, an actor

Steve Grey, a blue-eye

Georges Hackenschmidt,
a strongman

Diana Hart, a wrestler's partner

Bobby Heenan, a commentator

Hunter Hearst Helmsley, a heel

Hulk Hogan, a blue-eye

Les Kellett, an iron man

Kendo Nagasaki, a masked man

Mucky Mal Kirk, a heel

Ilona Kirk, his widow

Klondyke Kate, a heel,
an accident waiting to happen

Johnny Kwango, a head-butt
specialist

Ken Livingstone, a politician

James Mason, a blue-eye

Vince McMahon, an American promoter

Mick McManus, a heel

Paul Merton, a comedian

Shawn Michaels, a blue-eye

Miss Linda, a blue-eye, a valet

Mitzi Mueller, a blue-eye

Sir Atholl Oakeley, a blue-eye,
a promoter

Jackie Pallo, a heel, a promoter

Jackie Pallo Junior, his son,
a heel

Steve Prince, a heel

Pat Roach, an actor, a blue-eye

Rollerball Rocco, a heel

Lloyd Ryan, a drummer,
a manager

Mal Sanders, a heel

Jimmy Savile, a broadcaster,
a blue-eye

Davey Boy Smith, once a
blue-eye, now a heel

Adrian Street, an effeminate heel

Tony Banger Walsh, a heel,
a grass

Kent Walton, a commentator

The Reunion: 'I only want pleasant things to happen'

1

'That fat bastard – I could kill him!' said Jackie Pallo

Simon Garfield: In August 1995, more than 150 professional wrestlers gathered at a pub in Greenwich to talk about how things used to be – a reunion. They looked all right apart from the ears, but their walking was terrible, and when they got up to order a drink you saw that many had bad limps or ruined backs. It was like a reunion of people with hip replacements. A friend of mine took a group photograph; we positioned some of them outside the pub in several rows, with some kneeling at the front, and Mick McManus looking like the team captain, and when we finished a couple of them had to be hoisted to their feet because their knee joints had shattered.

It was Wayne Bridges's pub. Wayne's other name was Bill. People had come down from Scotland to attend, and it turned into the biggest single gathering of wrestlers there had ever been. I was told that whenever wrestlers get together they just sit around and lie to each other, but it wasn't all like that.

Pat Roach: Now the photo's done it's time for the roll of honour, lads. It's wonderful that we're all together. I'm thrilled to bits. It's time for our dearly departed who have gone before. We've got a list. If we miss anyone out we'll talk about them after.

Big Bruno Elrington, Johnny Kwango, Frank Joyce, Bob Joyce, Tony Mancelli, Peter Maivia, Bert Assirati, Johnny Dale, Tony Carr, Lou Marco, Sam Stone and, bless his heart, Catweazle. Was anyone here at Catweazle's funeral? Wasn't it just the most wonderful funeral you've ever seen in your life? A very brave man. Count Bartelli, Frankie Blake, Steve Clements, Roy Bull Davis, John Foley, Alan Garfield, King Kong Kirk – Mucky Mal Kirk, Mike Marino – bless him – Archie O'Brien, George Relwyskow. Can you imagine George saying to Archangel Gabriel, 'You're my pal. Me and you are going to do it together.' Tibby Szakacs, George Drake, Jack Dale, Bill Brennan, Dave Armstrong, Johnny Lipman. Just this week, gentlemen, Zimba passed away. Very sad, now Honey Boy's gone and all. That's what I've got. Now you. Now don't all shout at once, so we can hear the names.

The Wrestlers: Ken Cadman! Dean Briscoe! Alan Dennison! Ian Campbell! Bill McDonald!

Pat Roach: No chance that Jim Breaks is dead, is there? Now here's someone else who would like to say a few words.

Mick McManus: Ladies and gentlemen, lovely to see everybody here again. A marvellous turn out, and what a day. A special thanks to all the fellas who have travelled a long long way. Thank you to Wayne and the organizers Tony and Joe.

Joe D'Orazio: I like to think we should all be friends now. There was a lot of jealousy back then, and people didn't have nice words for each other. But now I want only pleasant things to happen. People say they didn't like McManus, but we got a lot of money from McManus. Because people went to see McManus we got a job on that bill as well. People didn't like Pallo – a lot of people. But because Pallo worked that night, we all worked that night. We're all brothers now.

Kent Walton: It's a lovely occasion seeing all these old friends, but I've been shocked by a couple of them. Wayne Bridges, the way he turned when he walked really worried me. And Vic Faulkner told me, 'I've got to watch it, every morning I have to get up slowly.' And he was one of the most agile athletes I've ever seen. Now Tug Holton – it took him twenty minutes to sit down in the pub, with two sticks. It was a relief when he managed it. He had a brain tumour as well. He was in a hell of a state. George Kidd – I think every bone in his body had been broken at one time. He had one calf smaller than the other. Everything about him resulted from this game.

Do you remember Johnny Czeslaw? One of my favourite people, great sense of humour, lovely showman and a beautiful wrestler. And tough with it. He's now in a hospital permanently, can't see. He had a brain tumour; the front of his head sticks right out, and he sees shadows. I said, 'Shall I go and see him?' and they said, 'He wouldn't recognize you.' That's a result of his time in the ring.

And someone like Alan Dennison, who died just after a match at Southport . . . These are fit men, at the peak of their skills, and then, suddenly, not.

Joe D'Orazio and Johnny Kwango: 'So he became a wrestler like his mum'

Mick McManus: Johnny Kwango died recently, but not during a fight. Of cancer. He did the flying head-butt. I went to his funeral. He lived in Peckham. Nice funeral. Well, silly thing to say, 'nice funeral', but it was very well attended. His real name was John Lagey. He joined the African ballet, but his mum said it was undignified. So he became a wrestler like her.

Kent Walton: Mick I see more than anyone. I like these reunions because it saves having to chase up people that you don't want to spend too much time with. At the reunions you've got three or four hours with nothing else to do but meet people.

Jackie Pallo: I don't see many of the old luvvies. I've pissed some of them off. If anyone ever has a go at me about wrestling I say, Look, I made it, I know everything there is to know about wrestling, I've been there. I was a big, big star, the biggest, and I dragged Mick up there with

3

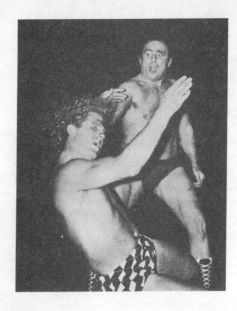

Mick McManus attacks Jackie Pallo: 'The whole fight he just kept nutting him'

me. He'd admit that. They used to go potty for us when I fought Mick. Why? Because we were both very good. You can't beat the quality. Mick had that know-how: a great performer. Horrible bastard, but a great performer.

I've seen him three or four times in the last ten, fifteen years. We were like pros, like double acts who don't talk to each other. Laurel and Hardy hated each other. It's a job. When you're finished, you're finished. Never been in Mick's house, and Mick's never been in mine.

My Uncle Tom keeled over while watching me and Mick in the ring. We were on TV, and he was up in Sunderland. He died during the match. Terrible thing, but that was the sort of heat we generated.

Mick McManus: I haven't seen Jackie for about a year. His book soured a lot of people against him, but he's all right. Had his hips done. The book actually had very little impact. The public are very strange. They only believe what they want to believe. People used to come up to me and say, 'Do you really get hurt or is it all fixed?' Some nights I'd say, 'It's all fixed, obviously.' And then they'd say, 'No, no, of course it's not.'

4

Jackie Pallo: Half the stuff in *You Grunt, I'll Groan* we had to cut out for legal reasons. People didn't turn against me just because of that book, it was much much earlier. By the time the book came out the average fucking moron knew it was bent. It's like asking a jockey does he ever have any bent races. They're *all* fucking bent! You've never heard of a poor bookmaker, have you. With wrestling it just happens. It's a business. But I never damaged a wrestler with that book. I wrote it to get back at the promoters.

Max Crabtree: Jack actually went insane with the job. He needed psychiatric treatment. Jack wrestled for me all over the country. The problem was that bitterness crept in. What happened was that you can stay around too long. He had a glorious run in wrestling, and he was a real superstar, such a good servant. Jack would go anywhere, and he's never ever let a promoter down. But unfortunately things changed: nothing is forever.

In the case of Jack, he was getting older and he'd been seen and been around a long time. Once the halls would be full to see him, but it ended up where people saw his name as the main event and they wouldn't come. They'd seen enough of him. When a wrestler is wanted every night, there's only so much he can give. Banging about, sweating, travelling. And in the case of Jack, the poor lad was burnt out and he didn't bloody know it.

His performances had got very suspect, very tired. He just couldn't come up with it. Jack was aware of it, but there was nothing he could do. And then he foolishly went and brought his son into the job. Jackie Junior was never ever intended to be a pro wrestler. In my opinion he hadn't got it. So it was like adding insult to injury when they went around together.

Jackie Pallo Junior: You know what killed it in the end? Big Daddy – this big fat man in nappies. People had seen Big Daddy belly-button people on the floor for ten years, and you had to be a complete moron to think there was any credibility left in the damn business.

Max Crabtree: Jack didn't like my brother Shirley, who you'll know as Big Daddy. My brother was having a lot of success, and every-where Jack went people would say, 'Bloody hell! How ya keeping

Jack? Have you seen Big Daddy – ain't it marvellous?' Jack would say, 'That fat bastard – I could kill him!'

Jackie Pallo: But that's the past. I retired twelve years ago when I had my hip done. I was fifty-eight and now I'm seventy. And at seventy I can say that the only thing that's straight in life . . . is death. Everything else has got an angle.

2

'So that was the ears business,' said Mick McManus

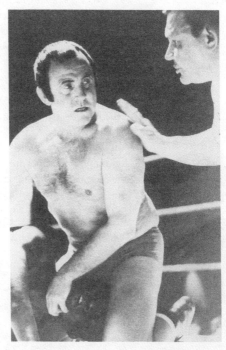

Mick McManus:
'The thickness is just blood that's congealed'

Mick McManus: These days I play golf all year round. My handicap's eighteen. I do pro-ams. I do a bit of public relations for a company called Anixter. They're in the distribution of wire and cable and various networking systems, and I look after some of their clients on golf days, dinners and lunches, that sort of thing . . . I'm taking some people in February to St James's Palace which is nice. In March it's the eve of an England rugby game, a dinner. So, you know.

The Terrible Turk, CB Cochran and Hackenschmidt: 'There was a nasty sounding crack'

I got into it when a friend who runs the company said, 'Come and do some work – I'm sure people would like to see you at the exhibitions. They'll all remember you.' He was right.

I was a big star in the sixties and seventies, when it was on the television. We used to get regular audiences of six million, and then the idiots who decided what was what on TV said it was too downmarket for them. I find that a bit laughable really.

Simon Garfield: Mick McManus travelled to the reunion from his flat in Denmark Hill. His apartment was warm and chintzy, furnished with fat sofas and porcelain figures and gloomy landscapes in oils. In the lounge there was a portrait of the wrestler by John Bellany. It was as abstractly splashy as much of Bellany's colourful work, and could have been any one of two hundred aging men walking around Clapham that day. 'Not a bad likeness,' Mick told visitors. Antiques are a passion of his. When he came off the television with wrestling there was a gap of a year or two, and then he started popping up on a lot of antique shows.

Mick McManus I used to love the crowds, especially the way I'd wrestle. I used to get a kick out of manipulating the hordes. I'm not being big headed, but I could really bring them up and drive them mad and then tone them right down, keep them quiet and sort of wrestle sometimes, not doing anything particularly bad, just wrestle nicely and it was like waiting for the other boot to drop, they never knew when I was going to start doing something which I shouldn't do, something which they didn't like, something which they could scream and shout at.

I used to feel good about that. Even at the end, in my fifties, I used to like to feel that I was still good enough to pull them in.

Simon Garfield: The first thing you noticed was his ears, the way they seemed solid and swollen, three times the thickness of the ears on ordinary people. Then there was his physical stature, bullish and still rather menacing, his lungs like drained beer kegs. He walked around slowly so as not to crash into things, but you couldn't help wondering if he didn't spend a lot of time breaking and then replacing his figurines.

And then there was his hair. For several decades the one question everybody had about professional wrestling was, 'Is Mick McManus's hair fixed?' You could spend hours trying to work it out. His hair seemed not to have changed in thirty years, always flat and firm and brushed forward into tiny spikes at the sides, forever tar black with no grey, the Dracula look. There seemed little doubt that it was not his natural colour.

Max Crabtree: Believe me, when the wind blows there's not much there. I travelled all over with Mick, and he ended up working for me. He was complex. He didn't like it when people made fun of his size. We'd be walking down Princes Street and people would come up to him and say, 'You are, aren't you? You're Mick McManus!' The next thing they'd say was 'Bloody hell, I thought you were bigger than that – you're a little bugger aren't you!' At this point Mick would say 'Fark orff!' He liked having someone like King Kong Kirk with him to ward off any trouble. But Mick would shake their hand, and he had hands like a woman. In British wrestling, the body beautiful side of it was never very big.

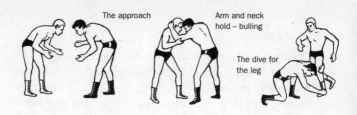

The approach

Arm and neck hold – bulling

The dive for the leg

You look at Mick. He was full of bloody cysts.

Mick McManus: People used to say it was fixed, but you should have seen the injuries. Sometimes it was impossible to get out of bed the next day, because you were battered so badly. I didn't enjoy that and I didn't like waiting on railway stations at Crewe, like at one o'clock in the morning waiting to catch the train to King's Cross or Euston. I used to get knocks and torn ligaments, shoulders and ankles. You'd have to take a week off but you knew you'd recover.

I broke my collar-bone and my wrist falling out of the ring. And the cauliflower ears were so painful, people don't ever realize. Cauliflower ears are caused by the breaking of little blood vessels in the ear and the ear fills up with blood. A single blow can do that. Or when you see rugby players, especially fellas in the pack, in the second row or something, it's the rubbing and bending of the ear. By bending it you break the blood vessels inside.

That's why you see a lot of rugby players now with headbands. It keeps the ear back so they don't get the bending. It was a surprise it was so painful because it's only blood. You could have them drained, the blood drained off and flattened out, because they became a nuisance. But then unless you really rested for a long time you knocked them again and then they'd fill up again, so really it was a combination of draining off a lot of the blood and hoping the rest would harden and congeal. That's where the thickness comes in. The thickness is just blood that's congealed, just solid blood. So that was the ears business.

Max Crabtree: Even when he was at his height in the ring, Mick McManus also had what was called the office hold in London, that was he did the datesheets, the matchmaking. If you annoyed Mick, you might find you only got two dates in February.

Mick's background was that of a printer. Mick was a good pro-

Waist lock from rear

Block for waist hold

Waist lock from front

fessional, one of the all-time greats of that period. The other boys knocked him, but fuck what the boys said. They wanted him out because they hated him. He was successful, the public liked him, arses on seats. He annoyed them. Most of the other boys just couldn't do it. They thought they could. But they weren't like Mick.

Mick McManus: I was born in the Old Kent Road. I left school when I was sixteen, nothing special. I joined this weightlifting club and the fellow who used to run it was called Fred Unwin, a strong fellow and a part-time wrestler. He said the best thing was to join an amateur club and get to the learn the basics. So I joined the John Ruskin in Walworth, and I went there for about a year and I learned. I never won any championships or anything, but amateur wrestling is the best training you can have.

The key to wrestling is that you've got to have a pretty strong neck. There's no submissions in amateur, so it's all a question of pinfalls, of just touching the shoulders to the floor. To get the advantage you had to get behind the fellow so that you could take him to the ground a lot easier, and then have the possibility of turning him over. In order not to be pinned, if you were going to be turned you tried to go into a bridge and that way you're stuck on your neck so it had to be bloody powerful.

In training you pushed and pulled around just to get the feel of things and to build up the muscles, just shoving and pushing the other fellow, and he would do the same with you. I remember doing that with Freddie Mills the world champion boxer, and he thought it would be easy because he was so fit, but he got absolutely knackered so fast. Wrestlers use a different form of muscles.

Then of course you learned the various moves and throws and holds, and how to distribute your weight. That was the other key: how to balance, how to fall right. I was about seventeen. By that time I realized that I liked it, and thought perhaps I'd try and get a

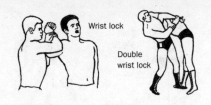

Wrist lock

Double
wrist lock

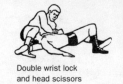

Double wrist lock
and head scissors

living out of it. I went to see Les Martin, one of the directors in the Dale Martin group, and I said, Any chance of a match? I knew that pro was a lot more exciting than amateur.

Peter Blake: The first match I ever saw my mum and aunt took me. Just after the war there was an enormous need for sport, and after they'd been to Bexley Heath Drill Hall a couple of times they said to me, 'You'd probably enjoy it, come with us.' It was about 1947. I'd go to art school during the day, and then come home and go to wrestling with them in the evening.

It was a small hall, packed, with a ring in the middle. We used to stand in the corners, almost under the ring. In the interval you'd go and have a cup of tea and piece of cake, all very innocent and nice. On that very first bill was Mick McManus fighting a wrestler called Al Lipman. I don't think I saw Lipman again, but of course McManus went on. It was all black versus white in the moral sense, and I fell in love with this wonderful theatre. There were people I am sure who were convinced that it was a genuine fight to the finish.

Mick McManus: I've still got the marks on my head from a lot of fights. I had loads of energy, all this power inside me, something I was born with. Some people are born with weak eyes or partially deaf, but I just happened to always have bags of energy.

I think you could say that a lot of my fights thrilled the audience. In letters I got people used to say how hard I was . . . secretly they admired my style. They told me to drop dead and all this business, but I meet people now and perhaps they'll say, 'Cor blimey I remember you, used to drive my mother mad on Saturday afternoons, oh God she used to carry on about you but she loved it and she wouldn't miss it for any money in the world.'

Women did seem to like it. First of all, in my experience, women are always a bit bloodthirsty. They're not always the demure type,

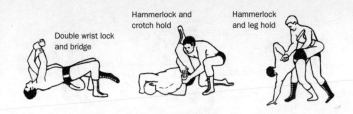

Double wrist lock
and bridge

Hammerlock and
crotch hold

Hammerlock
and leg hold

they like a little bit of blood and thunder. If you go back to the old days of the old guillotine, you usually found women in the front rows, they weren't always hiding their heads in shame at the back. And of course they probably used to identify with us wrestlers, maybe looked upon the young ones as their sons or those a bit older as their lovers. God knows what they saw in me. They just used to hit me.

There was a certain sexual attraction, because a lot of the fellas were nicely built and looked good. Wrestling was also something at which you could really let yourself go. You could scream and shout. No one ever took any notice, because it was the norm. If you went somewhere else, they'd say 'bloody lunatic'. But in people like me they could perhaps see the traffic warden or the income tax man, the foreman at the works or the governor or all the nasty people. There was a therapeutic value, I suppose.

It was a sport which was entirely different. It was what I call a low-budget sport, not terribly expensive and quite within the bounds of people, whatever they earnt. At the ringside, the ladies would be running up. I used to make sure that I didn't get too near the ropes, otherwise someone came up and banged you on the head with a shoe or a bag. If you get banged on the head with a high-heeled shoe, especially with the heel, it can give you a nasty lump. And although they used to think we were superhuman, you still feel pain.

Peter Blake: I felt a kind of affinity with McManus, and after one fight, when everyone was screaming at him, as he walked back from the ring I said, 'Nice fight, Mick!' and he said to me, 'How you going, son?' as though he knew me. I remember it now, so I think I must have been quite touched.

I liked to support someone who was always a villain, never anyone else's favourite. McManus had a lot of arrogance and there

The standing headlock

Counter throw to standing headlock

Hip throw

was something genuine about him, certainly a strong wrestler. You felt that if it genuinely turned into a fight, he'd win.

Simon Garfield: McManus would never denigrate the game or expose its secrets, but everyone who talked to him about wrestling seemed to find him obliging. He enjoyed taking you through the photographs he'd collected – Mick and the celebrities of the day. And he would prepare a four- or five-page history lesson in blue biro, a brief outline pulled from books or the chat over the years. It began with the observation that wrestling was the oldest sport in the world – Greeks, Romans, all of that. He liked to mention that wrestling was the sport of kings, practised by Richard the Lionheart, and that Henry VIII wrestled the King of France on the Field of the Cloth of Gold.

Mick McManus: Wrestling became popular in the USA in the mid-1800s. William Muldoon was the first official world champ. The wrestling was in travelling sideshows with challengers from the ground. The American Civil War interfered to some extent, but in 1861 it came back and did very well. 1900–14 was the golden age of wrestling. It became the major sport in the English-speaking world, dwarfing boxing and other sporting activities. In the years 1899 and 1900 the British music halls had strongman acts with Sandow and Sampson – these were very popular but after a while the interest waned.

Jack Carkeek, a Canadian Cornishman, travelled the music halls giving wrestling exhibitions and made a steady living. At the Alhambra Theatre in Leicester Square he was challenged by Georges Hackenschmidt, the Russian Lion, a very impressive wrestler and strongman. For whatever reason, Carkeek refused the challenge. But CB Cochran, an impresario, was impressed by the Russian Lion and became his manager.

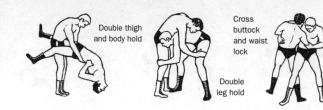

Double thigh and body hold

Cross buttock and waist lock

Double leg hold

Simon Garfield: Most of the protagonists are no longer with us, but their memoirs make much of the impact Hackenschmidt had on the public's imagination and their own fortunes. CB Cochran met him at the Hotel Cecil (subsequently the Shell-Mex building in the Strand), where the Russian revealed 'the most perfect specimen of physical manhood' he had ever seen. He did a few handsprings. He had 'the smooth rippling muscles of a greyhound' and a slender waist. But he was 'as depressed as only a Russian can be', and determined to leave London immediately. Cochran persuaded him to stay, and set in motion what even modern-day wrestlers refer to as the match of the century. Even wrestling in 1904, myth was everything.

It became known that Hackenschmidt had won tournament after tournament all over Europe, and was probably the finest Graeco-Roman specialist the world had seen (Graeco-Roman, unlike the 'all-in' style that succeeded it, allowed only holds above the waist). Cochran set him up at the Tivoli for £150 a week. We learn that he broke all box-office records.

Charles Cochran: All London, all England, had gone wrestling mad. Wherever one went, wrestling was talked – in bars, clubs and at family parties the mystery of the 'half-nelson' was discussed, coats were taken off and demonstrations, more or less inaccurate, were given.

One night, at the Canterbury in the Westminster Bridge Road, Antonio Pierri, an old wrestler who had been known as the Terrible Greek, arose from the stalls in company with a giant who wore a long heavy fur coat and a Turkish fez. This man, said Pierri, speaking from his place among the audience, had come to this country for the express purpose of proving Hackenschmidt to be an impostor. He was Ahmed Madrali, the Terrible Turk, the favourite wrestler of the sultan.

 Leg trip  Half nelson  Half nelson with arm and leg

For days the newspapers were full of Hackenschmidt and Madrali. Many discussions took place, and ultimately the match was made in the office of the *Sportsman*, to take place at Olympia on 30 January 1904. I had given what was at that time an enormous purse for a wrestling match, £1,000 for the winner and £500 for the loser. I have the two cheques, passed through the bank, hanging framed in my office.

Sir Atholl Oakeley: Everyone was sure that the Turk would end the Russian's long list of fast victories, and the house was sold out long before the day of the match.

Charles Cochran: Such an audience, fashionable and representative of all classes, had never before been seen in England for a sporting clash . . . high-school mistresses, country parsons who came to admire a perfection of form that comes perhaps once in a century. Hackenschmidt himself had been influenced by Pierri's propaganda, and I have never seen a more nervous man than he was as he paced up and down his room before the contest.

At the call of time, Madrali very slowly moved towards Hackenschmidt with his hands stretched out before him. Hack rushed at him like a tiger, got him under the arms, encircled his body with a grip of iron, lifted him shoulder high and threw him on the ground with a thud that sounded like a sack of potatoes falling. But there was a nasty-sounding crack. The Terrible Turk lay on the mat with his arm broken. It was all over in a few seconds. It was on that night that the story originated that a spectator, having just taken his seat, stooped down to pick up something he had dropped, heard a shout and as he straightened up the match was over.

When Hack retired from wrestling he devoted his life to philosophy, writing an enormous book which he published in German and English. At his request I arranged a meeting for him with

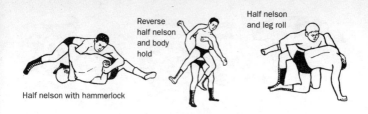

Reverse half nelson and body hold

Half nelson and leg roll

Half nelson with hammerlock

George Bernard Shaw. They talked for a long time and Shaw subsequently wrote to me that although he could not quite follow what Hackenschmidt was driving at, he 'got the decided impression that he was no fool'. When I last saw him he was living in the south of France, and though I hope it is not true, William Bankier told me that he had heard from a reliable source that Hack was doing forced labour for the Germans.

Bill Abbey: Cochran ran another big show in 1910 at Crystal Palace. Unlike the Hackenschmidt–Madrali fight, this one lasted for a while. It was between two heavyweights, a big attraction. One was much lighter than the other and didn't have the power, but he had lots of technical wrestling ability. The other fellow wasn't a great wrestler, but he was heavy and difficult to beat. They went into the ring and they hardly made contact, sitting it out for four and half hours. The crowd were bored stiff. They ended it when it got dark. After that, the wrestling generally went downhill.

Mick McManus: The business dropped off from 1910 to the outbreak of war in 1914, which sounded the death knell. After the war wrestling became popular again in the USA, with men like Ed Strangler Lewis, Toots Mondt and Jim Londos. This must have stimulated interest in the UK because in the early thirties it became very popular, with thirty-nine regular shows running in Greater London.

Simon Garfield: 'All-in' was introduced to Britain in December 1930 by Atholl Oakeley, a professional wrestler turned promoter. Previously a man could only be defeated if his shoulders were simultaneously held down for a count of three, but Oakeley had noticed that many heavyweights developed their bodies until they were oval, making them impossible to pin. So new holds were introduced, many below the waist, and submission moves

Half nelson
and top scissors

Fall from half nelson
and top scissors

Start of leg split

appeared for the first time. A wrestler could now lock his opponent with his legs or arms in such a way that escape became impossible or pain unbearable. The moves had novel names: step-over toe hold, crooked head scissors, Japanese leg-lock. With these, Oakeley observed, 'No longer was it necessary for a man to look like an ox in order to be champion. The crowds flocked in.'

The new rules carried an extensive list of fouls:

a) kicking with the toe or instep;

b) kidney punch or any form of direct knuckle punching involving the third phalanges of the fingers;

c) striking in the groin or abdomen;

d) horizontal pivot punch;

e) elbow in stomach when bridging;

f) hammer lock with bar, flying mare with palm uppermost, strangleholds, throttle, choke, carotid-artery lock;

g) knee in stomach;

h) gouging, finger-wrenching, scratching, biting, hair-pulling, ear-twisting, hair-plucking and spitting;

i) striking the referee, seconds, officials or members of the audience;

j) oiling, towel sweating, anaesthetics on the hair or clothes, resin or the use of pepper or any noxious drug;

k) throwing the opponent out of the ring over, and without touching, the top rope;

l) failing to apply submission holds gradually, i.e. jerking so as to try to cause an injury and/or death.

Bill Abbey: There was such demand for men when all-in wrestling got big before the war. The kingpin of wrestling in the North was George Relwyskow, the Olympic lightweight champion of 1908.

Completion of leg split

Front bar hold

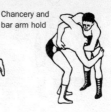
Chancery and bar arm hold

George was bringing up all sorts of men from the South to wrestle in his main venues – Leeds, Edinburgh, Sheffield.

My second eldest brother wrestled for him. His name was Leonard Alfred Abbey, but when he turned professional in the thirties they called him Jack Dale the Brixton Bonecrusher.

George viewed my brother as a reliable fellow, which many of them weren't, and asked if he knew of anyone in the South who could ensure that his wrestlers got on the train to reach his northern venues on time. Often they'd go out on the drink and perhaps wouldn't bother. He would never know whether someone he had booked was on the way to Leeds or not.

Our family wasn't doing that well at that time, so my brother suggested my father. This was 1933/34. The arrangement was that if my father couldn't get them on the train he'd find a substitute. Moving on from there he began doing a little promoting himself, at the Tufnell Park Palais de Danse. When I was ten I was first taken there by my mother, and we used to come back with my father. A big night out. We used to sit on the danceband stage, a small balcony, and the smoke that came up was poisonous. The biggest names at that time were Bert Assirati, the British champion who wrestled open air at the Ring, Blackfriars. Then there was Lane's Club in Baker Street, well run, the mecca of wrestling, a bit like a nightclub. The big draw there was Bob Gregory. There was Atholl Oakeley who became a Sir, one of the few genuine titles ever in professional wrestling.

Sir Atholl Oakeley: London gangsters once came into my dressing room at Brixton. 'We have bets on –,' they said. 'Tonight you will lose.' Threats and requests to lose matches had always amused me. Whatever could be said of other professional sports, no leading fighter in those days ever took a dive in any wrestling match.

Bill Abbey: The big stars were people like Jack Pye and his brothers

Escape from
chancery and
bar arm hold

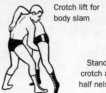
Crotch lift for
body slam

Standing
crotch and
half nelson

Harry and Dominic, who wrestled at Belle Vue, Manchester, and the Liverpool Stadium, and Francis St Clair Gregory who wrestled in the Cornish style. Then Izzy Van Dutz, who was billed as a Dutchman. Came from the East End.

My father's business expanded, and he was on his way back from looking at a hall in Birmingham when he was killed in a car crash. This was in 1935. My eldest brother took over from him, and he found he could earn a lot more promoting wrestling than as a tallyman for a coal company.

My brother began producing all-in shows all over. All-in wrestling wasn't licensed or controlled in any way. There were rules, but few kept them. There were many unsavoury and abusive things. By the outbreak of the war people had objected to the abuses, and it had almost collapsed in disrepute and disarray. There were women wrestling, blatant punching and gouging, strangulation holds. People could be kicked in the testicles.

Mick McManus: It became a victim of its own success. What happened was that it became so popular just before the war, and there were so many shows running, and everybody who could find a hole somewhere wanted to put on a show. The supply of what you might call good wrestlers, those who had a good knowledge of wresting, was a bit limited. So consequently some of these promoters didn't care who they used as long as the fellow was perhaps a bit big or ugly or fat, and could just go in there and make a few sounds and do a bit of punching and kicking. Unfortunately there was perhaps more of that taking place than actual wrestling. The problem was that you can't suddenly learn wrestling in a couple of weeks or so. Most matches ended in brawls both inside and outside the ring. So wrestling was banned in London just before the war because it was so shambolic.

When it came back in the forties it came back very cautiously,

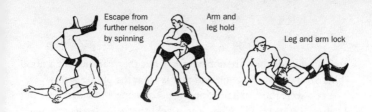

Escape from further nelson by spinning

Arm and leg hold

Leg and arm lock

and it was mostly drill halls and baths halls, swimming baths boarded over in the winter. Genuine promoters tried to resurrect the sport but found councils and hall-keepers anti-wrestling. In 1946, Norman Morrell, a former Olympic wrestler and promoter, met with Lord Mountevans, Commander Campbell, a member of the radio Brains Trust, and the MP Maurice Webb, and between them they thrashed out a set of rules to govern professional wrestling. It took off again, but in a controlled manner.

Sir Atholl Oakeley: Nearly all the great competitive heavyweights of the pre-war era seemed to have vanished. While all wrestling promotions with which we had been connected had naturally been closed down when war broke out, others had taken the opportunity to promote in our absence. Some promotions were being held under Mountevans Rules, an abbreviated copy of our all-in rules of 1930. Lord Mountevans, as 'Evans of the Broke', had achieved worldwide admiration. Yet here was this man, a peer of the realm, apparently filching our rules.

After travelling north to find out what was going on, I was told that wrestling was now being run as a closed shop, with rights of admission strictly reserved, so eliminating outside challenges. I bought a ticket for one of these so-called tournaments and saw at once that none of the four matches was genuine. Although billed as 'contests' they were obviously exhibitions. An amateur could have seen through all of them. Competitors escaped from Boston crabs. One threw his opponent to the ground and then stood back as he got to his feet. Another jerked his opponent's wrist. His adversary at once turned a somersault.

'What's that throw supposed to be?' I asked the MC.

'Oh, that was the Irish Whip,' he replied.

I said, 'You must be joking.'

Afterwards the promoter said, 'We have lots of men. Perhaps by your standards they are not wrestlers but they can put on a good show with plenty of action and that is what the public wants.'

'Very well then, what happens if someone buys a ticket and accuses you of fraud? What if it is held that your bouts are billed as contests but in reality are exhibitions?'

'I never said our bouts are exhibitions. If anyone said that they would have to prove it. Anyway, what's wrong with exhibitions? I take the view that, so long as we give the public plenty of action, they won't grumble. Exhibitions are not a 'fake'. 'Fake' is when you bet on the result of a fight when you know that one fighter has been paid to lose or has been threatened with violence if he doesn't take a dive. We don't arrange our results. We pay our boys good wages. What they do is up to them. We don't want to know. All we ask is a good all-action show.'

'If results are arranged the press will find out. You know how the papers hate wrestling.'

'What can they do? Some wrestler with a grouse may tell them a tale. If this happens and an article appears, a week or two later everyone will have forgotten it. No one believes what they read in the papers.'

'And the position of television if they take it up?'

'We can cross that bridge later. If we ever get on TV it won't be your kind of wrestling. It's much too slow. All that sort of amateur stuff is old hat. Modern people want action.'

Dropkick

The splash

Forearm smash

Boston crab

3

'Let's pray to God he doesn't die,' said the promoter

At the Royal Albert Hall: Bill Abbey (*far left*), The Duke of Kent,
Max Crabtree (*centre*)

Royal Albert Hall Programme Note: Many are the highlights that
stand out when one looks back to 1948, the year in which Dale
Martin became a limited company. That they were able to promote regular wrestling seasons here at London's historic Royal
Albert Hall, all the while maintaining such a high standard,
speaks volumes for the technical skill and enterprise without
which such deeds could never have been attempted, much less
accomplished . . . certainly the standard of wrestling we shall
expect to see will owe much to the efforts of your promoters who

have made it their business to spend a lifetime giving the wrestling public exactly what it wants.

Joe D'Orazio: In 1948 Dale Martin had one of those great old gyms that you don't see anymore, terrible smell of sweat, sawdust, big signs up saying 'No Smoking', and everywhere there was this stench of cigarettes and butt-ends on the floor. Dales had moved into 313 Brixton Road, the centre of the empire. It was from there that they transformed the business, always put on strictly good shows, people who could wrestle.

Bill Abbey: Dale Martin consisted of my family – now all known as Dales – and Les Martin. Brother Jack had wrestled for Les, and my brother Johnny ran some charity shows with Les during the war. When that ended they did more at Beckenham Baths and the Agricultural Halls, Maidstone, and from there it just grew. They asked me to come along one night to be cashier at the door, and gave me £2, good extra money for someone working at the Prudential. I joined them full-time in 1950 when I was twenty-five, two years after Dale Martin had formed. My brother said, 'We think we can make a real go of this wrestling.'

Suddenly it seemed like a terrible decision. Shortly after I joined, the Chancellor raised entertainment tax to 25 per cent, and we were having a terrible time. To keep it orderly we needed great adminis-tration and very tight controls. The LCC came to every show and filed reports. On one occasion we were a man short and had to find a last-minute replacement. So things were running late, and the MC kept the crowd entertained by telling jokes. He said, 'I understand there's a captain here from the Salvation Army who specializes in saving wicked women. Would he please save one for me.' We got an angry letter from the LCC telling us not to tell stories like that. The height of absurdity.

We were in what seemed like constant conflict with the wrestlers. We didn't pay them much, and when things became hard we had to fight their demands. So we formed Joint Promotions with the other wrestling companies, basically to keep other pro-moters out and control the wrestlers. With Joint Promotions we developed our own territories. Dale Martin had the South,

Relwyskow/Green had Scotland, Morrell/Beresford had the North and Best/Wryton had the Midlands and parts of Lancashire. We agreed not to poach venues, and not to operate within a ten-mile radius of each other. If the wrestlers didn't turn up they would get their remaining dates cancelled. If they went off to fight for other smaller promoters, we threatened them with never working for Joint Promotions again.

Max Crabtree: There were a few wrestlers who were still in the ring after the war, like the Pye Brothers and Bert Assirati, and Vic Hessle, father of Bert Royal and Vic Faulkner. It was a very closed shop, and some of the wrestlers were extremely sloppy – unprofessional.

Joint Promotions came about because the wrestling was in disarray. Someone like Jack Pye, a huge villain, would get a call from Norman Morrell saying, Can you wrestle for me in Blackburn on Sunday? and Jack would say, Yes. Then someone like Arthur Wright would ring up and say, Can you do it for me at Ardwick Stadium in Manchester? and Jack would say, Yes. Then he'd accept something else, which he had no intention of keeping. He'd just go to the one where he'd get a pound more, or which suited his other commitments, and the huge crowds that had heard he was coming at all the other venues would be disappointed and almost revolt.

The wrestlers were all working one promoter against the other – lunatics taking over the asylum. To counteract this the promoters ran what was basically a closed shop. They'd just share wrestlers between them, offer each man a monthly date sheet, and if he honoured it he'd get more but if he didn't he'd be out.

Bill Abbey: We were threatened with the Monopolies Commission on a number of occasions, but we always fought it off because it was never worth their while doing anything. It was probably illegal, but we stuck to it and that was that. Everyone hated us for it, especially the wrestlers.

Joe D'Orazio: I was very suspicious of the formation of Joint Promotions, felt it was unfair. So I supported the wrestlers' attempts to form unions, and wrestled for the other promoters who hadn't been asked to join – but good promoters, because I never worked for rubbish. I did it because I genuinely wanted to be free, and not dictated to. I wrestled a lot in Belgium, France and the big German tournaments: if you went against Joint Promotions you had to go abroad just to get the work.

I helped with pickets and all sorts of protests outside Dale Martin shows. I began promoting by myself – the Poplar Baths, the King George Hall in Glasgow – but we couldn't get the standard of wrestlers we wanted, so gradually we started to work with Dale's. We had to. After a while my shows faded, and I started working for Dale's full-time as a referee. I said I would never wrestle for them again, but refereeing was okay. They were very good to me, considering I began as an agitator.

It was Billy Dale who told me Charlie 'Spider' Mascall had died – he was the historian of wrestling, he knew what I know now, only forty years ago. I was asked to take over his old jobs, doing the publicity and programmes and writing for newspapers. I wrote the programme notes for those big Albert Hall shows. So I became a Dale backroom boy, working in the office, under the name of Bob Scala. Scala is my real name – Giuseppe Scala. Another name I had was Mario Muldoon.

I also did some work in films, as a wrestler and as a stunt double for the Charlie Chan character actor J Carrol Naish – I did about thirty films. Every time Charlie Chan fell down stairs it was me. I painted and wrote poetry, and *Aquarius* did a feature on me, on which I read out one of my poems, 'The Wrestler's Lament':

> I'm just about fed up with this game,
> With its bumps and its bruises and bangs.
> The dear sweet old ladies in front rows
> Sharpening their claws and fangs.
> The soft fat man with his blonde girlfriend
> Who jabs with his lighted cigar butt,
> The bald-headed vulture
> Whose battle cry is 'Why Don't You Get Your Hair Cut?'
> Those wicked old mums with hatpins
> Ready to maim and kill
> Umbrellas at the ready, wielding stiletto heel.

Types our dear forefathers would have burned at the stake:
Pencil-necked youths with long black hair,
That greet every fall with 'Fake!'
The jeering, shouting, ignorant lot
Smelling of smoke and rain
I wish they'd jump in the river,
Then I could pull the chain.
The din, the clamour, the peanut shells,
The microphone booming above it,
I'd leave it tomorrow I would I would,
But the trouble is: I love it.

That's one of mine. I once got attacked by a fan of Mick McManus. I'd disqualified him, and two thousand people thought he was right to go, and one didn't, and he came at me. I saw him and hit him first, and it was all over the local papers, but no court action.

The closed shop brought some very dodgy promoters, people who had no idea how to run a show, perhaps former wrestlers thinking it was easy money. Out in the sticks I've seen things you wouldn't credit. Some promoters would advertise, say, McManus, Haystacks and Pallo. You'd turn up, and it would be Charlie McManus, Ron Haystacks and Sammy Pallo, and what could you do?

Many promoters put on shows with no hope of getting the big names to work for them, so they made things up. One man announced a big name for the top of his bill, and you knew he couldn't even pay that man's train fare. Just before the main event the promoter would come out and tell the audience, 'I don't know how to tell you this, but I've got some very bad news for you now. I don't know how to tell you, but there's been a big car smash. The top of the bill was in it, and very badly injured. Let's pray to God he doesn't die . . . And while we're at it, let's have a collection for his wife and children just in case.' Of course there was no car crash, and the top of the bill was probably at the pictures in London, never contracted to fight that night. So the promoter put the collection in the office, and went on to wrestle 'in his place'.

Gentleman Jim Lewis's Announcement: We formed the Wrestlers'

Joe D'Orazio:
'You'd turn up,
and it would be
Charlie McManus,
Ron Haystacks
and Sammy Pallo'

Welfare Society because a wrestler has got to get on his bended knees to some of these promoters if he wants to get a square deal. Our object is to secure the independence of our members against a promoters' syndicate which handles most of the fights in this country. The syndicate pays fees which we consider unfair and a measly share of what the promoters earn. If a fighter has a complaint he has no one to go to, and the promoters just don't want to know.

Bill Abbey: Everyone was looking for new stars. Les Kellett turned up at Norman Morrell's gym in Bradford and said he wanted to turn professional. When someone new came in you always tried them out with someone very tough to see how they handled themselves. Les was put in the ring with a man who wrestled for us in the South as Arthur Belmont, but in the North was Arthur Belshaw, one of the Belshaw brothers of Wigan. Arthur was heavier than Kellett and soon had him in a submission hold. He had Kellett's arm, and said to him, 'Submit or I'll put it in plaster.' Kellett refused to submit, and just said, 'Break it!' So he gained some respect for that.

Adrian Street: When I started with Dale Martin's, against Jackie Pallo, I got £5 main event. I thought that was pretty good, but they made me give 10 per cent back to a so-called manager they made me have. Then the week after it went down to £4. I was married with a kid and another on the way. I could never afford cabs, so when they dropped me off in Brixton after a match I would walk all the way to Kensal Green. Whenever I asked for more money I was told, 'Oh, the time isn't right.' But times were great. Dale Martin's were running six shows a night. The audiences were enormous, and the wrestlers were practically being starved.

Brian Dixon: Dale Martin knew that it had a monopoly and all the major venues. Their philosophy was, 'Keep them hungry'. Keep them hungry and they'll keep on fighting. Otherwise they'll be wealthy men and get blasé and they won't do it.

Bill Abbey: The money started to roll in when a new Chancellor came along. He was a cricket fan, and he was appalled at what the entertainment tax was doing to the game. So he removed the tax and by the mid-fifties our business was transformed. We simply couldn't put on enough shows. Ten shows a day wasn't unusual, afternoons as well as evening, new venues all the time.

Milo Popocopolis's Announcement, 1955: We will play fair with the promoters if they will play fair with us. Some of them are pocketing £500 for a night and hand out tenners to the wrestlers. Wrestling plays to houses of 7,000 at places like Belle Vue in Manchester, but the average purse over the whole country is only £15. Apart from wages, we want to make sure that boys who turn professional are of some standing in the game and have proved themselves as wrestlers before they fight for money. We don't like the haphazard ways these boys can come in now. We are dead against the blubber-and-bounce boys who just move around the ring making noises and faces. In our view wrestlers should look like wrestlers – they should be clean, fit, athletic and dedicated to their job.

Joe D'Orazio: It was billed as the biggest fight: Bert Assirati, who had spent the last four and half years in India, and the Ghoul, who was a huge draw in England, a masked wrestler, six foot four with enormous hands. Assirati went to India because he couldn't get enough work here – the best heavyweight there was, but frozen out by Joint Promotions when he decided not to fight for them. Meanwhile, in his absence, the Ghoul had become one of Joint Promotions' biggest names. So this was the showdown. I was the referee.

The promoter was old Bill Shelton, who's dead, long dead, or else I wouldn't be telling you this. It was taking place at the back of the Merry Fiddlers pub in Dagenham, on the football pitch.

Come the big night it's pouring with rain. There are thousands of people showing up with big umbrellas, the take is enormous. I'm in the dressing room with Bert, and I'm taking a photograph of him. I go out for a cup of tea, and this fellow comes through dressed like the Ghoul, only he's six inches shorter than the Ghoul. The crowd all start shouting, 'Fake! Fake! It's not the Ghoul!' And of course it's not – it's nothing like him.

I told Bert that it wasn't the Ghoul, and he said, 'I don't care who it is – I'm going to kill him.'

At this point I know that Bert will kill him if he can. I know the exact move. He's going to grab his legs, and then it's a natural reaction for any wrestler to grab Bert's chest, and then Bert will straighten up and fling him in the air and land on him, eighteen, nineteen stone . . . Crash!

I thought that the crowd would then lynch the so-called Ghoul and kill him for wasting their money. So fearing the worst I arranged for a couple of fellas to put the Ghoul on this door that was lying off its hinges, and rush him straight to hospital.

Half way through the first round, after Bert had finally caught him, because the Ghoul had just been running round the ring trying to escape him, Bert gets that hold on him just as I knew. The real Ghoul may not have fallen for it, but the impostor did. Crash! Bert wins the fight, and the Ghoul rolls out the ring onto the floor, groaning in pain. The crowd are trying to attack him, but I'm standing across him to protect him. About ten minutes of fighting. I get some support from another wrestler, Frankie Hughes, who had just come to watch the fight.

The door I organized can't get through. Eventually an ambulance comes, and the Ghoul is stretchered off to the Dagenham Hospital. I tell another wrestler called Charlie Big Boy Scott to follow him, and take him his clothes and see he's all right.

Meanwhile, the promoter had escaped with the takings. Bill must have been almost eighty, used to wear a big black coat with a homburg full of dust. He had a big red nose, so we called him Rudolf.

Big Boy Scott followed the Ghoul to the hospital, where he still had his mask on. Apparently there had been a big scene in the ambulance when they tried to take it off, and he was fighting them off. He was still groaning at the hospital, but he was all right to be moved. He was probably thinking the crowd would come looking for him, so Big Boy Scott put him in his car, drove him to St Pancras and got him away. The Ghoul got no wages, and we never heard from him.

A week later I called up Bill Shelton, pretending to be Scotland Yard, saying, 'What happened to all that money you took away from those people?' He nearly had a heart attack. Then he said he'd come round with my fee, and he brought it round, and my wife made him a plate of spaghetti. I took him to the bus stop for his journey back. The next day he wrote me a letter. Said that when he got home his toilet had frozen up.

4

'Oh dear, an accident, not to worry,' said Les Kellett

Brian Glover:
'I can't be doing with
Masambula'

Brian Glover: You've talked to Mick? Mick's rich now. And he knows a lot, but I suppose his dad wasn't a wrestler like mine.

My dad's real name was Charlie Glover, but he wrestled as the Red Devil. My mother used to crochet his masks – they were good, other wrestlers asked her to make some for them. I've often said that I wondered what our neighbours thought on washing day with all these red masks flapping on the line.

He used to take me to watch him at the Ardwick in Manchester. And often he finished up with this bag full of copper, as sometimes he did promoting as well, and I counted it all out on the train back home.

My dad ran a gym in Barnsley, and I went there first as a boxer. Totally the wrong shape – too short and my hands weren't long enough – but I was the perfect shape for a wrestler.

I was a child of his second marriage. They didn't get married until I was nearly twenty. He came down to the gym – I was punching the bag – and said, a very moral man, 'Now me and your mother made it right today.' I said, 'About bloody time.' He said: 'There's no need to swear.'

He was in the gym the night he died. He'd retired by then, but the promoter Norman Morrell brought big Shirley Crabtree and Max down to Barnsley, and my old man was showing off. He was pulling some weights, and had a heart attack and died that night. A fellow called Wildon Shephard, the Lincolnshire Farmer, took him home. I went down to see him, and he said, 'Take my groin off', wrestling slang for ring: we always used to say, 'Get in that groin, lad.'

My dad, he could hardly read and write. He taught himself. He was a bright guy, but he had not been greatly educated, a bit of a gypsy. I was twenty-one and he was sixty-eight.

I was schoolmastering. We had National Service, stationed in Grays, Essex, and I remember going down on a pass to Southend. I'd be on 28 bob a week in the army, but I'd get £8 off Matt Moran at the wrestling booth. Going back and buying an entire hut a Naafi meal.

It was my main source of income for twenty years. I began as Erik Tanberg, the blond bomber from Sweden. I couldn't open my mouth, of course, or the game would be up. As Erik I got people in. And once you got them there, the show was always about next week, about setting it up so they'd return for the rematch. But one night Leon Arras, this Frenchman, didn't show up, so I went on as him. The promoter said not to forget I was a Frenchman, but soon I became Leon Arras from Barnsley, so I could talk real, and the name stuck.

Years later, I got a call when I was wrestling in Rome. It was the real Leon Arras, old by now. He ran this bar in Rome, and we ended up arm wrestling in it, on French telly, for the real Leon Arras's name. Who won? Moi! He let me. The reason he didn't show at Wilmslow was because his wife wouldn't let him travel – didn't trust him.

There were lots of women if you wanted them – ring rats we called them. Not always young or great looking, but always there. I used to tag with Bobby Graham, and we used to wrestle in Spain for months at a time. His wife always used to ask, 'What's that funny sound when you're going down the driveway together? A high-pitched screeching sound.' The answer was, it was Bobby going 'Yipppeee!' – away for twelve weeks of mayhem, leaving her with the off-licence they had.

In Spain they never want to lose. They're the big hombre and they say they've all got relations in tonight. Wherever you went the same guys had relations – in Seville and Barcelona and Madrid. The promoter was saying, 'Listen, the Inglese has got to win, because he's back here next month with so and so.'

I was still on the way up when I went on *Coronation Street* – two episodes. I sold Stan Ogden his window cleaning round, and that made me top of the bill. Then there was *Kes*, big in the business, but Ken Loach has always been a bit arthouse and the public didn't really see it.

In 1971 Trevor Nunn asked me to play Charles the Wrestler in *As You Like It* at Stratford. It was me versus David Suchet as Orlando. It was a great fight, the best choreography – the classic Shakespeare technique of a big opening spectacle and then you've got them. I remember Eileen Atkins saying, 'You can't follow it.' People were attacking us with umbrellas from the audience.

In the middle of the run the phone rings. It was Tiger Ted Beresford, the promoter, a pal of my dad's. He ran Leamington Spa, not far from Stratford. He said, 'You're going top of the bill with Masambula tonight!'

I said, 'Ted, I'm with the Royal Shakespeare Company, I'm a very posh actor. I can't be doing with Masambula.'

He said, 'Someone's dead. I want you there. Your dad would have been there.' It was like the mafia speaking, an obligation, a blood tie. I had to go. I did the scene in the play, kept the gear on – designed by Farrah, this beautiful leather costume, quite unsuitable for a long fight – drove to Leamington Spa, wrestled Masambula, and lost again. Rushed back to take the curtain call, as if I'd just gone out for a fag.

I wrestled Les Kellett many times. And he wrestled my dad. The big story was that fight against Norman Morrell, perhaps you've heard it. Morrell was another promoter, a strange little man, we called him Adolf. He said he had met Hitler. So Norman and Les are wrestling on the mat, and when you're wrestling for real and someone grabs your finger, you've got to submit or else they'll break it. Morrell gets hold of it and says, 'Finger, Les!', and Les goes, 'Break it!'

We hung around together a bit, though he wasn't what you'd call social. That little scar on my top lip – Kellett gave me that at Doncaster Corn Exchange. Someone had wrapped the ropes in red, white and blue plastic, American style, and Les ran my face down the plastic and it bled for a day.

Max Crabtree: Les Kellett wrestled for me hundreds of times. He's eighty-two, I reckon he'd be eighty-three now. Still around. God I lost some of my hair carting Les round. Les is a very complex man. He was a bit like Pagliacci the clown. The man behind, off the scene, was not the man that was in the ring.

Ninety-nine per cent of the lads were shit scared of him. Physically shit scared of him. Les knew that, and Les knew how to use it. I'm being brutal now. Les was the sort of fellow you wouldn't want living next door to you.

He was a very, very hard man. The guys who were on with him, because they feared him, he absolutely made them look like

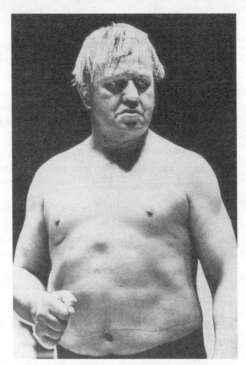

Les Kellett: 'He had hogs and things'

rubbish. And they couldn't do nowt about it. Oh God, I've seen times . . . you see he didn't make it until he was fifty-eight years old. Most fellows at fifty-eight can't walk, let alone wrestle, but Les was that hardy type. He had ten glorious years when his body was wanted every night, here, there and everywhere.

His whole persona was hard. He had a small farm only about five miles from where I am now, up in the Brontë country, up on the Moors, and it was . . . awful. There were no lights, only paraffin light. There were old mining shafts there, and water – they had to get it out the well. There were bloody ducks in the house. He lived hard. His whole thing was that: if there was an easy way and a hard way, Les would take the hard way. As a result of it, of course, he was a great character, I don't want to knock the fellow. But when I think back now, he was hard work.

Yes, Les would do that thing with the finger: Break it! You can't

37

comprehend it . . . he'd be sat in the dressing room and have no trunks on. He'd have his wrestling boots on, but not his bloody trunks. He'd have one of those hats on, and his glasses, and be reading a heavy book, and he'd be hoping that one of the young wrestlers would say, 'God you do look a bastard without your pants!' But most people wouldn't speak to him if he had the hump on. He was that forceful a personality. I remember when he came into the dressing room . . . many a young lad made the mistake of thinking that Les was a nice fella outside the ring. And Les *wasn't* a nice fellow outside.

Joe D'Orazio: I remember Les once in Birmingham, when somebody barged in the dressing room. Now a dressing room is a private place. I wouldn't let fellas bring their girls into dressing rooms – Get Out! But this fella just comes in and asks Les for an autograph, says something like, 'Sign here, if you can write.' Les got this bloke's head under his arm, and got it right up to the electric fire. Burnt all his own arm as well. The fellow was screaming.

Jackie Pallo: Les? Hard. He won't talk to you. He doesn't want to know.

Jackie Pallo Junior: He didn't want to talk to people even when he was around. With Les there was this remarkable transformation in the ring – this laughing, funny man doing the wrestling, and then the minute the fight ended, boom, he was gone. Dad and I are two of the few wrestlers he ever spoke to.

Jackie Pallo: If he wanted to, he'd smash you up.

Joe D'Orazio's Programme Note, 1967: What can you write about this man who has been a champion and yet is still dismissed by many wrestling patrons as a clown? Should some of his moves in the ring, executed with such apparent ease, cause you to be amused, it would be well to think awhile of the timing, the skill and the wrestling know-how that went into that very move.

Take that fantastic tip-up in the ropes with which he gets so many falls. An accident was the birth of that one. Thrown against a very slack set of ropes, Les went out backwards, landing on his head. He had plenty of time to ponder over his mistake, six weeks in fact, in a hospital bed. One quiet Sunday afternoon the hospital ward was shattered by a loud cry of 'Eureka!', and Les Kellett had found the secret.

The day he left hospital he went straight to a gymnasium (complete with a plaster collar) and put his idea into practice. It worked. In hospital again at the beginning of this year, he won't tell you why but I will; it was to have a very large abscess removed from his buttock, caused by body-slam after body-slam. The doctor's final words were, 'Go and have a good holiday.' He did – in a gymnasium. He asked keep-fit fanatic Alan Dennison to give him a treadmill workout, and was very cross with him for making things too easy the first day.

A son of the soil, he has cows to attend to, rabbits which he breeds for fur and meat, battery hens to feed and various jobs of work that keep him busy about his farm. A busy man, yes, but he still finds time to give a helping hand to any youngster thinking of making a career in wrestling.

Bill Abbey: We asked him to give someone a try-out at the Dale Martin gym in Brixton. He wasn't best pleased with that chore. The new wrestler had been fighting for a rival in the South, small-time, and now wanted to move up. Within forty seconds Kellett had dislocated his shoulder and had him screaming on the canvas, and wouldn't let go. He had to be forced off. The fellow was taken to King's Cross Hospital by ambulance.

Max Crabtree: Les ended up buying a transport cafe in Thornton Road, Bradford. To put it bluntly, it was a shithole. I used to pick him up there. He lived down in the basement.

Margaret, his wife, God bless her. An Irish woman – how she could live with Les, God knows.

That cafe would open up at six in the bloody morning to serve transport people. It was the most crude . . . Les had built the tables, he had those big banana fingers, Les. If ever he got hold of you . . . It was awful. I used to call at the cafe for him. He used to come up from the cellar. He had a few animals in the yard at the back. They were in terrible order.

Oh God, the stuff he'd done. He, oh . . . he believed in the occult and all that stuff. He would go days and wouldn't speak. You just knew you didn't mess this fellow around. It was a physical thing. I've seen him take guys down up and down the country, not in wrestling.

Les Kellett was originally Norman Morrell's referee. Les has refereed Bert Assirati. He wouldn't soldier in the wartime. It was his personality. He spent a lot of the time in the nick. He wasn't a thief or anything like that – it was him going against the establishment. He were full of fire. He would wrestle when the war was on.

Wayne Bridges: I was one of the very few people he'd talk to. He called me Beau Brummel, because he thought I was always so immaculate. We travelled together a bit. He was very hard, it was true. I was at his house in Bradford when he was threading a wire through a cork and missed and threaded it through the web in his hand, between his thumb and forefinger. Blood everywhere. He said, 'Oh dear, an accident, not to worry,' and he poured a bottle of iodine over a ball of cotton wool, and put it on the needle, and then threaded that through the same hole in his hand. It was bleeding all the way in the car to the hall. We stopped at a garage on the way to get some sticking plaster, and that didn't stem the blood either.

Adrian Street: Les was reluctant to have the image he had. I've been with Les before now, and people have come up to him and said, 'Les you were so funny I almost peed myself,' and he would get very offended. He always preferred to be known as a hard man than someone who was funny.

He was a very nasty man, actually. A lot of the stuff he did was to intimidate other wrestlers. A lot of the crowd didn't understand what he did. I've thrown him on his face outside the ring, out onto bare concrete. He's gone down and he hasn't even tried to protect himself with his hands or arms. He got back off the floor and he had pieces of loose concrete embedded in his face. That was not to impress the people – that was to impress me. And I wasn't impressed because I thought he was a fucking idiot.

I've known Les . . . he had hogs and things. Do you know the story of when he got his hand bit? He was talking to a friend of his on the farm, feeding the hogs, and this big old boar bit him on the hand. He got an infection and his hand swelled up like a boxing glove. Instead of going to the doctor's like a normal person he was wrestling that night, so he goes to the show.

In the dressing room the guy he's wrestling with says, 'Don't go in the ring and wrestle like that.' Les goes, 'Yes, yes, I think you've got something there . . . I can't go in the ring and wrestle like that. So what I'm going to do to get rid of the poison is put my hand here, on the ground, and I want you to stamp on it.'

'Oh I can't do that, Les.'

'But you've just told me, and I agreed, that I can't go in the ring like this. So stamp on it, or I'll stamp on you.'

So this other wrestler stamps hard on his hand, and all this blood and poison and pus comes out of it. This is in full view of all the other wrestlers. He had to be the centre of attention did Les.

He could stand pain, all right. Going back to when he was one of Norman Morrell's henchmen . . . a big iron girder fell down onto Les Kellett's foot when he was working in Norman's gym. There was blood running through his boot. It took half a dozen of them to get the girder off his foot. They were running round saying 'Les, Les, are you all right?'

He said, 'We've got work to do – we'll look at it after.'

He was working there for hours before he said 'I think we should have a look at my foot.' They had to cut and tear his boot off, and there was congealed blood. It was for effect, and the effect worked because that was thirty years ago and I'm still talking about it.

Pat Roach: Les was working in London for a week, wrestling at Seymour Hall one night, Catford the next. Between these fights he was walking down the Haymarket feeling his sore neck and back, not feeling too good, and suddenly he looked up and saw a person who obviously had polio, dragging his distorted limb behind him, but with a big smile on his face. Les looked at that lad and thought, 'I ought to be ashamed feeling sorry for myself.' I love to remember things like that about people.

Max Crabtree: He still lives at that cafe. I could put you onto him, but it's . . . it's where eagles dare. You could just catch him right and he could be as nice as pie with you. But he could . . . You might be better writing to him.

There's not many round at eighty-three. Nobody took bigger bumps than Les Kellett. I've seen him go four rows back, upside down. If there were a narc in the hall carrying on, Les saw him and he'd be out over that top rope and land on top of him. He was fearless, took some murderous bumps. A psychiatrist would probably put it down that he was a masochist. I've seen him with the most awful cuts on his hands, most fellows wouldn't have wrestled with them, but he'd go in there. I've seen him with carbuncles up his backside. He was being run down. You can't wrestle every night – it gets to you. He'd go in the ring and say to his opponent, 'Slam me!' and most fellows wouldn't. He'd have three or four enormous carbuncles on his backside, and pus would be coming through his trunks. And people would be roaring with laughter. He'd be doing his funny antics. It would be enough to make you faint.

Simon Garfield, Letter 22 September 1995:

Dear Mr Kellett,

Please let me introduce myself. My name is Simon Garfield, and I've been in awe of you since I was a schoolboy. You always seemed to have a little more than most wrestlers – humour, strength, bluff and a vast amount of traditional skill. I've also admired your hardness.

I'm currently writing a book about British wrestling – its heyday and its decline. I'm particularly interested in talking to all the big names about their wrestling lives. I've met several important people thus far – McManus, Pallo, Bridges, D'Orazio, Haystacks, Glover/Arras – but my work would be incomplete without your knowledge and experience. I wonder if I could come up and see you for a chat? It would be a great thrill to meet you after all these years.

Please let me know when might be suitable. You can write to me at the above address, or phone me at any time. I do hope you can help – it seems to me very important to document what used to be such a thriving business.

With very good wishes,

Yours sincerely.

Brian Crabtree: 'I'll never wrestle again'

5

'So I got murdered,'
said Jimmy Savile

Max Crabtree: The top and bottom of it is, wrestling was the first and only thing that I enjoyed. There's nothing in wrestling that I don't know about in the period that I was involved. I totally lived and slept it. Some of the people you've spoke to, they were very shallow people. No knocking anyone.

I ended up running the whole scene. Mick McManus ended up working in the office for me. It was the best wrestling scene in the world.

Wrestling was the thing of my family. One of my earliest memories is of wrestling with my old man in front of the fire when I was three. Shirley's the oldest, then me, both in our sixties now. Brian is still in his fifties. My dad was also called Shirley Crabtree. Unfortunately my grandmother on my father's side was in the theatre, and she'd read the Brontë book *Shirley* and decided that no matter whether she had a son or a daughter that was what she would call it. It was a hard name to live with, and it made you tough.

My dad was a physical fitness fanatic and made a good reputation for himself in rugby league football, and went to Wembley in 1933 with Halifax. He was also a good professional wrestler.

My mum was a big woman, weighed fifteen stone. We lived with little money in a room three or four floors up, and she could carry sacks of coal up with no problem.

Shirley Crabtree: My dad's whole existence was based on his great strength. He'd go round bars and clubs doing a strongman act, bending bars and lifting people up. He would encourage us to join in the street fights to bring out what he called our 'competitive element'. He'd get us to go up to big chaps and pull them along the street. It sounds ridiculous, but we had to do it. He thought that being tough and winning was the only thing that mattered in life.

Max Crabtree: My old man buggered off and left my mum for another woman.

Brian Crabtree: Times were extremely hard – especially when our old fellow went. All around us were factories and mills and people clattering up and down in clogs through whirlwinds of soot. Mum worked in the mills from 7.15 am to 5.15 pm. In her spare time she'd work in the brickyards to try to make ends meet. She was frightened to death they would take us kids away from her and put us in a home.

Max Crabtree: Shirley went over to see Norman Morrell. He was already a big lad then, playing second team for Bradford Northern. But rugby wasn't his thing. He didn't like the idea of being in a team. He kept on getting sent off, and he was too aggressive, and I said to him, 'Better pack it in or one day you'll kill someone.'

So both me and Shirley started wrestling, and in the summer we were lifeguards at Blackpool as well. Shirley had one or two very good rescues and almost won the Mountbatten medal.

It was Norman's theory that wrestling was the perfect working-class sport. It was mostly men that came, few women and no children. In those days, it was always the heavyweights who were top of the bill, until George Kidd came down from Dundee as a light-weight, very fast and brilliant. They called him the Master of 1,000 Holds. There was no holds he couldn't escape from. People would pay to see him. He'd do an hour and get a standing ovation like Barbra Streisand. He later got a chat programme on Grampian. I think Jack Lemmon went on.

I learned very early that some wrestlers were stars from the beginning, and some would wrestle all their lives and never top the bill no matter how good. The public judged you, and wrestling

I am getting nearer to my goal,

(The Heavyweight Championship of the World) said Shirley Crabtree when he was interviewed after a recent fight. "I've had 15 fights and won them all. And, what's more, I have not conceded a fall."

Before he was Big Daddy: programme featuring Shirley Crabtree on beach

ability was only the half of it. Punters just didn't believe in most people. Most wrestlers were just one of the boys. We all wrestled, but Shirley was the one. Right from the start you could tell he was going to be the star.

Mat Review, January 1957: 'I am getting nearer to my goal (the heavyweight championship of the world),' said Shirley Crabtree when he was interviewed after a recent fight. 'I've had 15 fights and won them all. And, what's more, I have not conceded a fall.'

Max Crabtree: It was about being extraordinary. Even before television, before he was enormous and became Big Daddy, people paid to see him. Nine thousand paid to see him at a football ground.

Big Daddy: I had been wrestling as 'Shirley Crabtree, the Blond Adonis' and as 'Mr Universe'. I was well-muscled in those days and only weighed about fifteen and a half stone, but I realized that in wrestling, as in boxing, the real interest is in the heavyweights.

Max Crabtree: When I got out of the National Service I was as fit as a butcher's dog, and wrestling just took over our whole lives. I did it morning, noon and night for seven days a week. My wife? God bless her, I gave her five sons, and I was hardly home, travelling all over the country.

We all used to wrestle on the same bill, but Brian broke his leg unfortunately.

Adrian Street: I've known the Crabtrees since the late fifties. It was Max, not Shirley, who was the best wrestler of the three. Max is the only one I admired. Brian and Shirley were useless, never any good as wrestlers.

I was on the same card at Caledonian Baths the last time Brian wrestled. The three Crabtrees were on against three Hungarians. There was lightweight that Brian wrestled, a middleweight that Max wrestled and a heavyweight that Shirley wrestled. I was wrestling Leon Fortuna, and my match was the only one on the card that didn't feature either a Hungarian or a Crabtree. Brian got really hurt in his match, and I remember Shirley carrying him out over his shoulder and Brian saying, 'I'll never wrestle again.'

And he never did. He became a referee.

It wasn't long after that Shirley retired for the first time. In those days he was just another heavyweight on the card. Once they announced from the ring that Shirley was the British champion, and Shirley held up his hand. Then Bert Assirati stood up in the audience and Shirley nearly shit himself in the corner. Absolutely terrified, he kept on saying, 'If he comes in the ring, I'm getting out.'

Brian Crabtree: It was bloody murder. You'd get injured, and you never got paid when you were off. It was 'Let us know when you're right.' So I thought, 'Get into refereeing and you don't get injured and you work every night.' When you get older you get a receipt for everything you did when you were young. Your shoulder aches, your leg aches, you limp every now and again. I started in '58 and retired in '65.

Max Crabtree: I wrestled for Jack Dale, George Relwyskow, Norman Morrell, but I always fancied the business side of it. Initially I formed together with Paul Lincoln, Ken Joyce and George Kidd. We went against Joint Promotions, so we had to find a lot of our own wrestlers. I created stars – ask anybody. I brought a lot of people over from abroad.

Karl Gotch, an old-time wrestler from Belgium, rang me up from Florida and said, 'I have a little Japanese wrestler here and I know you'll like him.' I took him in the gym, and I rang Cyanide Syd Cooper up to come down and give him a go. Good pro, Syd. The moment he got in that ring, that Japanese boy, his whole charisma was right. I changed his name to Sammy Lee, from the name of Bruce Lee . . . I thought we'd put him down as one of the Lee family. I went over to a very good martial arts shop just over Streatham Common. I bought him this yellow outfit and I bought him this martial arts stick. We banged him on. Instant box office.

I brought in this guy, he'd been top of the bill at Madison Square Garden, Spirion Arion. I brought him in as the Iron Greek. Terrific attraction. Andy Robin in Scotland – what a great bloody attraction.

It was hard to find guys who were really committed. I lived

wrestling, but most of those lads you've been speaking to . . . You've been having a bit of nostalgia from guys who I'd send eight dates to in a month, and they'd cancel three of them, probably have a domestic problem with their wife for one of them, and you'd never be sure if they were going to turn up or not.

I've been invited to come to these reunions they have, but when I see who's there . . . If I'd asked them to get there for wrestling it would have been a bloody nightmare. These guys were fickle. They only thought they wanted to be in the job. If you get McManus level-headed he'll tell you the same . . . they didn't know if they wanted to shit or shave. They only wanted anything within five miles of home, provided it didn't interfere with their domestic life. But I worked every day, I had an office in Brixton and one in Leeds, and I spent my week between them, and then in the evenings I went anywhere in the country, any hall in any town where there was wrestling on.

Now Johnny Kwango, a great grafter. Now you're talking about a good pro. John you could rely on, he'd be in Torquay one night, then London, then the next bloody night in Warrington. He used to arrive at the hall in basketball boots, and he'd already have his trunks on under his trousers. Very athletic in the ring. His older brother, Black Butcher Johnson – Arthur Johnson – was another great pro. He's dead as well. His other brother is Cyril Lagey, who was in Sid Millwall's Nitwits. Do you remember that band? They used to do a novelty thing round the music halls, and Cyril was the drummer.

Harvey Smith throwing his man: 'Wrestling was all he ever wanted to talk about'

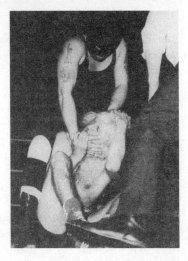

Jimmy Savile
(*on floor*) with the
Black Watch Beatle:
'He came on to "Twist
and Shout"'

John would delight the crowds. Every star does something different in wrestling, and it's that different thing that makes them stars. With Johnny Kwango the public loved the head-butt and the splits. But some of these would-be attractions just wanted to disappoint. Ricki Starr didn't want to do his ballet act after a while, he wanted to be serious, but that's not what the public had paid for. It's a business for God's sake.

I brought in Sky High Lee, six foot eight, a genuine American. Before he became a wrestler he was a heavyweight boxing champion and Frank Sinatra was his co-manager. Frank always liked boxing. Sky was a great villain. He used to ask women to throw darts into his back. He swallowed crushed lightbulbs. After one fight in Canada he went to a restaurant and the owner had taken such a dislike to him that he put rat poison in his food. He nearly died. At the hospital they told him it was only the bottle of whisky inside him that saved him. The restaurant owner went to jail.

Most wrestlers are always looking for the Golden Fleece. They believe that outside of wrestling there is a better thing for them. But usually it's not true. It's hard for wrestlers to come to terms with that. Like Brian Maxine. Brian wanted to be a singer as well, and he played guitar. But he didn't know whether to shit or shave. His songs were awful, and he always wanted them on when he stepped into the ring. All these guys, like John Quinn – it was me who went to Germany and brought him in. Giant Haystacks – I started him. These people didn't happen by accident. Somebody pointed them out and brought them to the front.

Jimmy Savile: I began wrestling by chance. I was the manager of a dance hall in Manchester in the late fifties when I got a call from a guy who owned the nightclub opposite me. He said one of the wrestlers had just died in the ring and they were putting on a benefit match, and would I referee? I said no, because I don't like trying things that I knew I couldn't do. But I said I would wrestle, because I was already doing judo and I fancied my chances.

I trained for six weeks. I was trained by Les Kellett and he gave up his evenings to show me a few holds and how not to fall on my head. When you hit Les with a forearm it was like hitting Leeds Town Hall. At the first fight the crowd outside were so huge that they were let into the club for free because the police feared a riot otherwise. And so I got the bug.

My proud boast is that I lost my first thirty-five fights. My first opponent was Gentleman Jim Lewis, the undefeated welterweight champion. Then I fought catchweight, which means you end up fighting any weight, including the most fearsome. So I got murdered. One very painful time, my goolies were kicked up into my body, and I had to go to Salford Royal. It was marvellous, because the most attractive lady doctor managed to coax my goolies out of my body. I finished off taking her for dinner.

I've had 107 pro fights and I covered Yorkshire, Scotland and Redruth. I topped the bill, obviously, because I wrestled as Jimmy Savile. I was desperate to win a match, but I was only fighting good people top of the bill, and there was no way they were going to go down to me. They all wanted to give me a good hiding because no one wanted to go home to their wives and say that a long-haired disc jockey had put them on the floor. For my first victory I feigned an injury in the ring, pretending I dislocated my shoulder. The guy then got very loose, and then whup, whup, whup, he wasn't taking care and I got a submission off him. He gave me a good hiding in the dressing room afterwards.

I was very very bad, but very enthusiastic. Out of the 107 fights,

I had 106 sellouts. The only time I didn't have a full house was when there was a bus strike in Huddersfield. I hold the record at Nottingham Ice Rink, where I tagged with Jackie Pallo. Jackie used to give me a good hiding, even though he was my partner. I got the cheers and he got the boos, so he used to crack me. He was a prima donna and a bad-tempered geezer.

The other guys respected me totally because I tried and wasn't afraid of damaging myself. I treasure that respect more than any pop award.

Max Crabtree: He wasn't bad, Jimmy. He didn't have the physical attributes, thin and wiry, but he was box-office magic. He had some very memorable matches with Cyanide Sid Cooper. Jimmy would put himself out for you. He entered to 'Twist and Shout'.

Harvey Smith was another very good turn. He was strong, and loved wrestling as a boy. He used to go to all the venues round the Ilkley Moors, near Bradford.

He didn't have to wrestle, but he loved it. We travelled all over in his top of the range Mercedes and wrestling was all he ever wanted to talk about. And he was good in the ring, strong legs, jutting jaw, loved a good scrap and the public loved him.

It was television that changed everything. Wrestling didn't need television, and had survived very well without television. You could say that when there was no television, wrestling was at its best. But Lew Grade had seen wrestling on television in America, and when he came back he knew that it was a very saleable commodity. Wrestling was made for television, the size of it, the bizarreness of it. Grade liked the razzmatazz. He really liked what it stood for.

Kent Walton: 'He got very uptight over it'

6

'Greetings, grapple fans,' said Kent Walton

Giant Haystacks: People used to set their clock when it began at four. The Saturday shopping ended before four o'clock. Shopkeepers complained that their stores were empty. For that one hour, everyone was joined as one in the UK, and it was something to talk about. We had better ratings than *Coronation Street*. Our own Queen used to sit up at four to watch wrestling. That is absolutely true. That came from the Duke of Kent.

Richard Crossman, *Diaries of a Cabinet Minister*, 12 July 1968: At midday I had to shoot off to Buckingham Palace for the first of our new-style Privy Councils. The Queen had agreed that after the formalities we should withdraw to the Caernarvon Room next door and have drinks with her. The Queen was in tremendous form. After the Council, when the drinks were circulating, she began to describe to me a television programme she had seen yesterday of a wrestling match, at which Philip had been present. An all-in wrestler had been thrown out over the ropes, landed on his feet, and after writhing in agony had suddenly shot back into the ring, seized his opponent and forced him to resign. She said what tremendous fun that kind of all-in wrestling was. 'Do you want a Royal Charter for them?' I asked. And she said, 'No, not yet.' It was interesting to hear what a vivid description she gave of the whole scene, writhing herself, twisting and turning, completely relaxed. It was quite an eye-opener to see how she enjoyed it.

Afterwards each of the Ministers had a good long talk with her alone before we all slipped off.

Mick McManus: TV wrestling started in 1955 and gave a terrific boost both for the sport and the TV companies. Viewing figures amounted to six and seven million. On a couple of Cup Final days Jackie Pallo and myself had a feud going and we wrestled just prior to the match and pulled figures of eleven to twelve million. It was accepted that more people watched us than the Cup Final.

Those figures were staggering, and they virtually murdered the BBC. And far less people had televisions then. The strange thing was that the BBC really could have had wrestling for themselves, because they had exhibition matches coming from Alexandra Palace in 1947. It would just be a mat down in a bare studio, no ropes, and a man would describe the holds: this is a cross-buttock, this is a flying mare, this is the counter to the flying mare and this is a full nelson. Then the wrestlers would put it all together into a match. Dead boring really, but they could have stuck with it.

On ITV, Kent Walton, a Canadian who hosted the pop programme *Cool For Cats*, was given the job of commentating. He had a very good voice that lent itself to the wrestling scene, as opposed to someone who was an Oxford type of bod that frequented the television companies in those days. But the problem was that he'd never been to a wrestling match before he got the job. So I took him down to a gym with a few others and we had to run through some holds and throws to acquaint him with what went on, what constituted a fall or a submission. He began that afternoon not knowing anything about it, but he was a pretty bright fellow and caught on fast.

What they didn't want was someone like an Eddie Waring. Remember Eddie Waring? 'Oh 'e's all right, 'e's only got a broken arm, he'll be up and about in two minutes.' They didn't want any of that, didn't want someone who would put himself over as a bloody comedy act, which Eddie used to sometimes with the rugby, much to the annoyance of rugby players. Rugby players used to get bloody annoyed with him when a fellow went down and took an awful whack and probably got broken ribs, and all that he's saying is, 'Oh there's no problem with him, he's a strong laddie, be up in a minute.'

Bill Abbey: I went along with my eldest brother John to see Ken Johnstone, head of sport at Rediffusion. Kent Walton had been doing the football commentary for him.

Kent Walton: I was handed a message. It told me to telephone Mr Johnstone at once.

'Hi Kent! What do you know about wrestling?'

'Wrestling? Not a thing. Why?'

'You'd better find out, boy. You're on – Wednesday.'

Johnny Dale set up a whirlwind tour of the country, showing me six full tournaments in a lesser number of days, and arranged for me to meet Mike Marino in the ring.

Suddenly it was Wednesday 9 November 1955. The time was 9 pm. The place, West Ham Baths. As the wrestlers entered the ring a blond-bonced fella slipped quietly into the vacant seat beside me.

Jackie Pallo: It is not generally known that Cliff Beaumont and I were the first two wrestlers to appear before the TV cameras. Unfortunately they were not broadcasting at the time. The camera crews needed a dress rehearsal for the first show, so Cliff and I went down to West Ham Baths and Cliff threw me about for an hour.

About a week before I met an actor, Kent Walton, at Rochester, and Mike Marino and I were asked to sit beside him and tell him what the boys were doing to each other in the groin. He asked me if I could do it on a permanent basis, while he learned his trade, and Dale Martin agreed to pay me a small fee. I did that for about eighteen months, and by then there wasn't any wrestling jargon Kent didn't know. He was even making up names himself for new moves.

Max Crabtree: It took you a while to get to know Kent, but he was a very committed, civilized man. A lot of people don't know who his wife is. His wife Linda was married to the late Leslie Grade, brother of Lew and Bernard. Her son is Michael Grade.

Kent likes a Guinness, and he's not a fighting man, but he did get upset when people said wrestling was bent. He got very uptight over it. It gave him a good living for thirty-three years. He ended up in bars after a match, bending someone's thumb back.

Paul Merton: Kent Walton always used to end each programme with the phrase 'Have a good week, till next week.' That was an ominous thing. It meant that this week you could have a good time, but next week . . . next week there might be a disaster. Only Kent seemed to know why. So you had to make sure you watched next week and the week after and every week after that, just to get his blessing.

Jackie Pallo: The television contract was rumoured to be worth £15,000 a week, which is very healthy when you consider that wrestlers were only being paid £25 at first, and later £40 for a TV stint. The most I ever got was £80 for a Cup Final day fight, and that was only because I did such a lot of heavy moaning.

At one time I was called aside and told that people had complained about my violent, villainous fighting, and that the junta didn't want me frightening families to death while they sat in front of the fire in their living rooms. It seems bloody daft when I think of the extent of violence shown on television today, but in those days everybody believed it was for real when you stepped on a geezer's nose and spun around.

Max Crabtree: We always had a fear of the IBA. The referee had to be seen to be in charge at all times. Certain holds weren't allowed. The wrestlers weren't allowed to show too much pain.

The anti-violence campaigners were very strong against wrestlers. And to a viewer at home . . . a lot of people got very upset when a baddie hit a goodie behind the referee's back. These wrestlers were professionals, they were showmen, but there would be hundreds of irate letters to the IBA from intelligent people who felt sorry for anyone who seemed to be in pain.

Robbie Brookside: We were told that if there was blood in the matches they wouldn't be shown. Any really abrasive moves like between the legs, was banned. Any swearing, any over the topness, it wouldn't be shown. In a lot of cases that's why people came to the wrestling – because it was controlled violence, and occasionally people would lose their tempers, and there would be blood.

Max Crabtree: When I took over I was brought to task almost every month. I had to go to London to account for last Saturday's show.

We had Mark Rocco on, and Mark was crazy. He couldn't help it. Mark believed that to be a good wrestler you had to dismantle the ring, hit the referee with the bell, throw your opponent into the audience. Nobody slept when he was on, but he was dangerous, because he could kill someone. So I kept on having to pacify the television people who said they didn't want him on no more, and I had to go back to Mark and say, 'Silly fella, you're off for three months.'

Kent Walton: Wrestling provided a TV programme that almost everybody went for. A well-known psychiatrist came up with a neat theory. He said, in effect, that wrestling showed men the type of man they would like to be, and women the type of men they would like to meet. Further, it displayed aggression in its purest form and a conflict between good and evil in which sides could be easily chosen. This conflict was so basic that almost every viewer could identify himself or herself with it.

Roland Barthes, *Mythologies*: Wrestling partakes of the nature of the great solar spectacles, Greek drama and bullfights: in both, a light without shadow generates an emotion without reserve . . . At such a pitch, it no longer matters whether the passion is genuine or not. What the public wants is the image of passion, not passion itself. There is no more a problem of truth in wrestling than in the theatre. In both, what is expected is the intelligible representation of moral situations which are usually private. This emptying out of interiority to the benefit of its exterior signs, this exhaustion of the content by the form, is the very principle of triumphant classical art.

Robbie Brookside: From the male point of view part of the entertainment is that they like to see the athleticism. I wouldn't deny that from the women's point of view they do like to see some ass.

Mick McManus: I suppose we really got the seal of approval when the royals used to come, Prince Philip and then the Duke of Kent. I once met Princess Anne at a charity thing. The man who introduced us said, ' . . . and this is Mick McManus the wrestler,' and she said, 'Oh yes, but I'm not used to seeing you with your clothes on.'

I remember going to Buckingham Palace with the Lord's Taverners to see Prince Philip, just to have a couple of hours up there. But at that particular time Franco had died and he had to go to Franco's funeral to represent the Crown. So Charles took his place. At that particular time Charles was at the Greenwich Naval College. I was introduced to him and 'Oh yes,' he said, 'you were at the Albert Hall last week.'

I said, 'Yes, that's right.'

'Some of the chaps from the college went along and had a jolly good show.' He said he couldn't go because he was on duty. I said to him, 'Well, your father went a couple of times and he enjoyed it.'

'Yes,' Charles said, 'he did.'

I thought afterwards I shouldn't have said 'your father', I should have said, 'His Highness Prince Philip went'.

Giant Haystacks: You'd be surprised who watches it. At the Albert Hall we had Roy Jenkins down one night. He's a big fan. Big business people came. And him who pissed off back to Cyprus – Asil. Petula Clark used to come. Savalas came. Charles Lawton once said, 'These men are the best entertainers in the world.' Peter Blake would travel all over to see it. People would ask Peter to come and give them an art seminar, pay him £10,000 to £12,000, and he just wouldn't go.'

I went to see Frank Sinatra sing at the Albert Hall. Because I wrestled there many times I knew the way out under the stage. I passed him in the corridor, with his two bodyguards, and he said to me, 'Mr Haystacks, I watched you on television this afternoon! I believe that British wrestlers are the best entertainers in the whole world!' We exchanged pleasantries, and he gave me his autograph.

Kent Walton: I've seen women have orgasms watching wrestlers. They're maybe getting on a bit, and maybe their husbands aren't up to it anymore, and so they get their pleasure watching these fellas on television and coming to the shows.

What made British wrestling so good was a combination of tremendous skill, speed, stamina, humour, showmanship – put them all together and you've got the Vic Faulkners, the George Kidds, the Les Kelletts. But without one you haven't got the others – that's what people forget. It's beautifully done.

Wrestling just became an institution. It was a fixture on *World of Sport.* Dickie Davies would introduce it from the studio every week, and you knew where you were – almost an hour of great, reliable entertainment.

I was so into it, with so many fellas I liked so much. There were only two men in the wrestling business that I disliked. After thirty-three years, out of all the hundreds and thousands of men and foreigners that I travelled with and met, only two. Wrestlers really help each other, especially with their injuries. I remember once seeing Johnny Kwango lying face-down on a piano at Brent Town Hall, with two people working on his back, trying to get him ready for the bout. And that wasn't supposed to be seen by me – how they were helping each other. They were supposed to hate each other.

I went in the ring myself, but not in front of the public. I went in many times with Mike Marino and George Kidd. My legs were buckled for ten days.

Dickie Davies: I couldn't stand wrestling. But it got us enormous viewing figures between four and ten past five.

Mick McManus: There were a lot of spin-offs from being a household name.

Here are the photos. Tommy Cooper. Obviously I got to meet Tommy Cooper once or twice at functions, and he thought it would be a good idea to do some sort of gag with the wrestling business. He got himself all done up in a leopardskin leotard, and we had a bit of fun, which looked a bit peculiar because Tom's about six foot four and I'm five foot six. It was a bit like Laurel and Hardy. It was just a wrestling sketch, and it probably ended with Tom winning. It was only short, because he had many different sketches in his show.

The Rolling Stones. That was taken at the Fairfield Hall when the wrestling was big big big and the Stones were only reasonably established, not the big shots that they became. At that time Brian Jones was with them. He was a nice little lad. He always used to say to me, 'Oh, you healthy looking bastard!' I went because my son wanted to see them and obviously I had no problem getting tickets from the Hall manager Tom Pipe. That evening Bill Wyman told me backstage that he lived in Beckenham, and I gave him a lift

Mick McManus's
photograph collection:
with The Rolling
Stones,
Prince Philip,
Harold Wilson . . .

. . . Rod Hull and Emu,
Tommy Cooper . . .

. . . Keith Fordyce and Cathy McGowan . . .

. . . Magnus Pike and Patrick Moore . . .

. . . Ernie Wise . . .

. . . and with Raquel Welch

home. He told me he had a lot of money, but he didn't know how much.

Raquel Welch. There was some press do, and some bod thought it would be good to do a Beauty and the Beast type thing. She was a great looker, didn't need those make-up people. She was a big shot then.

With Rod Hull and Emu it was a chat show thing that we were on. He's quite a nice fellow, but he can be a bit of a lunatic, he used to get very excited and carried away at times with this bloody ostrich. I said to him very quietly, 'Rod, don't get too excited or carried away, otherwise I might do your ostrich's neck a bad injury, which of course would be your arm,' because he had his arm up him, you see.

Jackie Pallo: If I wasn't wrestling on the box I was appearing on other people's shows. Dozens of them. My first TV acting part was on *Emergency Ward 10* when they featured an out-patients' unit and I was the wrestler who came in with a broken coccyx. A few years later I was in *The Avengers* as a grave-digger who had to wrestle with Honor Blackman.

What did Jackie Pallo have that most wrestlers didn't? Talent. Talent for a start. No one can knock me on that. The ability to do something on the spur of a moment and know what the public want. To make a little out of nothing. When I open a door, anywhere, when I enter a room, you know I've walked in. Doesn't happen to a lot of people. When I walk into a gents' toilet, everybody turns round and looks. Now more than ever, and it even happened before I was 'Jackie Pallo'. I have that sort of razzmatazz or whatever it is that happens. You go, 'Oh, who's this fellow?' Mick's got it, in a different sort of way. Les Kellett's got it. Wherever Les Kellett is, you turn and look at him. Certain people have got it. Unfortunately, not many. Thank God.

Adrian Street: Pallo is a sad guy. Jackie Pallo was never any good. He just happened to be on the first TV show that they ever did. He lost his match, but he lost it because he tried to dropkick someone. His opponent got out of the way, Pallo's legs went either side of the corner post and he mashed his Christmas crackers. Nobody had ever seen that on television before. It was his claim to fame, because everyone wrote in wanting to know how that poor man was. Then they kept on putting him on television and he became 'Mr TV'.

Jackie Pallo: If I wasn't doing daft things on television shows I was opening something, or judging beauty contests. I played charity darts, football and cricket and was good at going round with a bucket and getting the crowd to chuck money into it.

Robbie Brookside: The wrestlers all made a record, 'We All Go in the Ring'. They were all on it – McManus, Steve Logan, Johnny Kwango. The other side was 'Tiptoe Through the Tulips'. Top entertainment. They used to play it at the shows.

I didn't get on television for three or four years, and people assumed that if you weren't on television you weren't any good. But that's what happened when you wrestled for Brian. Brian never had much to do with television. He was trying, but the Crabtrees had the total franchise on it, a totally closed shop which meant that a lot of the best wrestlers were never seen.

Brian Dixon: I had a lot of meetings with the TV people, and they said that the arrangements they had were all fine and thank you very much. I finally got on after years of trying, but before that if you were in opposition to Joint Promotions, forget it. When I finally got a contract I was full of good ideas. 'Oh no,' they said. 'Kent Walton won't like that.'

Television was absolutely crucial for exposure, the shop window. It was rare that you got a very big crowd with anyone who wasn't big on television. The characters sold the tickets, and there were so many characters because of Kent Walton. If he said a wrestler was brilliant, then he was brilliant. If he said Les Kellett was funny, then he was funny. Les Kellett was a horrible person, as you will find out to your cost, but people laughed at him. You could not meet a more horrible person in your life. He was just horrible. But television has such an impact on people's minds. If you brainwash people enough, they believe it.

Adrian Street: The last time, Les turned up drunk. Previously, Les never ever drank or bothered with women. I was very promiscuous back in those days, and so were a lot of the other wrestlers, and he didn't like us because of that.

But Les suddenly started drinking, but big time. In the mid-seventies he'd go into a bar and all the other guys would be there, and the barman would come up and ask him what he'd have.

He went, 'Yes, I'd like a drink. What have you got?'

'We've got beer, whisky, brandy, cognac . . .'

'Give me a cognac. Not in that glass. Could I have it in a big glass like him with his beer? Could you put more in there. More, more, more.'

The barman would keep on filling, and Les would end up with a pint of cognac. He'd then drink this in one, as everyone looked on.

One of the last times I ever saw him he attacked me in the dressing room. I was in the shower room, and he was having a pee. I said hello and he didn't answer. I thought he didn't hear me. Then I said, 'Les, how you doing?' and he swung right round and threw a haymaker and it missed. He came after me and kept on throwing punches. Why I don't know. I kept pushing him away and I hit him once and he fell down in the showers. Then after he wouldn't wrestle. He was sulking. He said to Brian Dixon, 'Let one of these other superstars wrestle, let the superstars wrestle . . .'

I got no respect for him. He was a character, but he copied it all from Bernard Murray . . . all that falling backwards over the ropes, all of a sudden falling the opposite way to which you'd expect. Bernard Murray was doing that years before. He's a hard man, and he must have had an incredible pain threshold, but I always thought he was a prick.

Kent Walton: Les was very funny, a very good sense of humour, had me absolutely in stitches at times. But very hard, that's what people forget. He kidded around a lot, until he needed to, then crrrunch!

I think he used to have a caff in Bradford. I know he had a small-holding. I said to him, 'Les, can I be any use to you down on your farm?' He said, 'No we got special stuff for that.' Meaning special stuff. You know – manure.

Simon Garfield, Letter 7 October 1995:

Dear Mr Kellett,

I wrote to you a little over two weeks ago concerning the book I am writing about the history of wrestling in this country. Please forgive me for writing again so soon, but my urge to talk to you knows no bounds.

You are often in my thoughts, not least because so many other people I talk to have fine and funny and occasionally alarming stories about you. I need to know if at least some of these are true. I appreciate you must be busy with your animals, but just a little of your time would be most appreciated.

With good wishes,

Yours sincerely.

P.S. Several people tell me they can still feel the forearm smashes you inflicted on them.

Adrian Street with his father at his father's mine:
'Nobody was doing that before me'

7

'But then I got my image,' said Adrian Street

Adrian Street: The image was not my idea. Someone showed me a photograph of Gorgeous George when I started and I didn't like that gay look at all. But when I could afford it I bought these powder blue boots and trunks with the sides cut away. My jacket was powder blue velvet with big puffy sleeves and a silver lamé lining. I had my hair dyed blond, cropped on top and longer at the back. I thought I looked great, terrific tan, and when I walked out I thought everyone would say, 'Oh wow, doesn't he look good, what a great body and outfit.' Instead it was, 'Woooo Mary!' and the men were all saying, 'Can I see you later?' in these high voices with their wrists bent.

This upset me a great deal. I was really pissed off – I'd spent all that money. But I wanted to show them I wasn't hurt so I played up to it, kissing my muscles and making sure my hair was just right after a move. The reaction I got was tremendous.

Back in the dressing room the other wrestlers were a bit confused by it and thought maybe it was for real. And I used to mince and turn it back on them. I would wait until everyone else was in the shower and then glide in with the towel under my arms and go, 'Mmm, a smörgåsbord!' The place would empty.

Next hall I went to the same thing would happen, and again the next place. I was getting far more reaction than I'd ever got just by playing this poof. My costumes started getting wilder. In the beginning I would just wear a little bit of make-up, so that when I walked by on my way to the ring people would whisper, 'Is he wearing make-up?' In the end the make-up got more obvious, and I started sticking sequins and rhinestones on my face.

Up until then almost all the wrestlers had been hard, and if they weren't they pretended. But here was this 'poof' in their midst, and it threw them. The fans hated it, but you could see they were intrigued and I think the women were maybe a bit turned on. Nobody was doing that before me. Boy George wasn't even born when I started. And in the States, nobody painted their face before me, and nobody wore Spandex before I arrived on the scene. Hardly anyone had a lady valet. I'd make Linda carry my make-up and comb my hair and people hated my guts because I was treating a woman so bad. But then they also began to wonder what I was doing with a woman anyway.

The reason I was a success was because I would never come out and say anything either way. There's a guy called Adrian Adonis who started doing my gimmick in the States, and the first thing he did was say, 'I've got an announcement to make. I've come out of the closet – I'm a homosexual!' I watched him doing this on TV and thought, 'Well, you've just killed yourself stone dead.' With me there was a mystery – is he or isn't he? If someone asked me if I was gay I would say, 'That sort of accusation makes me want to scream.' Also, the reason it has worked for so long is that I'm a fucking good wrestler. I'm fifty-five.

Simon Garfield: Adrian Street took me round his new home near Pensacola, Florida. Here he ran the Bonecrusher Academy, a small wrestling school comprising a couple of rings (one inside, one out) and an apartment block where out-of-towners could spend the night. The apartment was decorated with his own paintings and walls of mirrors. 'Wrestlers like to look at themselves,' he said. 'You give them a mirror and they'll never be bored.'

The indoor ring was surrounded by photos of the men he had trained, in leotards made by his wife. There were many old wrestling posters. One said: 'BIG DADDY IS COMING'.

Street was proud to say that he still wrestled occasionally, and his image was now extreme. In some recent photos he looked like a vicious schoolgirl.

Adrian Street: I was born in Brynmawr in Breconshire. I left school at fourteen and a half. My dad was a coal miner in Wales for fifty-one years. The only time he wasn't a coal miner was when he was a prisoner of war of the Japanese.

The first thing I wanted to be was a Red Indian, then a gladiator. The closest I could come to being a gladiator was this business. I liked hurting people, and thought I might as well get paid for it. I was inspired by the American wrestlers I saw in magazines – Lou Thesz and Buddy Rogers and Don Leo Jonathan. That's where I got my first name Kid Tarzan Jonathan from.

The first live bout I saw was Bert Assirati versus Vic Hessle, Vic Faulkner's dad, in Newport. I thought the wrestling was great, but the characters were so dull. Everyone wore the same. Big woolly black trunks and little black or brown boots, but I was used to seeing all the characters from America.

I left home when I was sixteen and went to live in London on my own. I thought I knew it all, of course, and I went into gyms and saw all these blokes with cauliflower ears and bent noses and I thought I'd never end up looking like that. I'd always be far too good and fast.

They asked me if I wanted a pull, a pull around the mat, and they beat the crap out of me. In the bar later I had to hold my head up to drink my milk, because all the neck muscles had gone. I was trying to drink a pint of milk a day to build myself up, but it went all over my T-shirt.

I couldn't get a look in at Dale Martin's so I wrestled for people like Paul Lincoln at the Metropolitan, Black Butcher Johnson and Dropkick Johnny Peters. After about two years I got a letter from Les Martin saying I should come for a try-out. And the man they put me in with destroyed me again. Jack Dale took me in the backroom afterwards, and I thought he would tell me to get lost, but he said he was impressed with the show I'd put up, my resilience.

I slogged around for a long while, did okay, nothing special, the odd TV match. But then I got my image. Things began to take off for me as soon as I had that established. At the beginning a lot of the promoters said, 'Oh, you don't have to carry on like a queer,' but in time they realized what a draw I was for them.

My wages kept on going up and up. I went north and demanded more money, got it, and then demanded more down south saying I was thinking of moving up north. That worked until the early seventies when they got together and realized what I was doing. Most were on about £9 a night and I was on about £35 or £40.

When I first approached Bobby Barnes about forming a tag team he said, 'I don't know, I'll have to watch you first,' but then our Hell's Angels really gelled. When we started we had never even heard of the biker Hell's Angels. We just liked this idea of two opposites – angels who had turned bad. We came on like two choirboys in white satin capes, and our initials in silver sequins, and our silver hair over the top. Then when we got in we flung the capes open, and there were red sequins on the inside of our capes, and we had red trunks and boots – that was the 'Hell's' part of it. The crowd would go crazy.

Max Crabtree: Adrian was one of those misfits that was always involved with the intrigues of life. He never had the great success of a McManus, but he did register. But the promoters didn't particularly like what he did. He was a complex man. He liked to portray the role of a poof, but behind that façade, if one of the customers said to him, 'Get out of it you bloody poof, Street!' he'd be at them. He couldn't take it. And you had to watch him, because Adrian would do anything for attention. He would have shown his private parts on television if he thought it would have done him some good.

Adrian Street: I wrestled Les Kellett once when I had a new purple and lilac gown. Les was already in the ring when I walked out. Les's face dropped about a foot, because I came out and got a tremendous reaction to this gown.

He comes up to me and says, in his gentlest voice, 'May I, may I try your gown?' I said all right, because I didn't know what else to say at the time, and he had a great time with it, flopping it around, pulling lace off it. He stole the limelight and got the reaction back on him.

Couple of nights later I'm wrestling him again and the same

thing happens – great uproar for my gown, and he comes over to ask for it again. Only this time I say no. He was desperate. But I said, 'I didn't buy the gown for you – I bought it for me.'

Oh he was pissed. He went for me big time. If you were really frightened of him he'd knock the crap out of you. But to me Les wasn't superhuman. I was blocking him all the time, and he was growling like a dog. I started singing, 'Who's afraid of the big bad wolf'. He started to laugh, and we then had a normal match.

Dave Soulman Bond: Yeah, the image thing. The Soulman name came about as a result of a discussion between myself and the promoters. I went to America for a while, and I got the hat. One of those floppy hats that Kool and the Gang had. Just that, and the cape and a little swagger can get the crowd going.

Some of the other black wrestlers did have a bit of what you might call the negro-type role. The black guys were well-liked with their tribal outfits or whatever. Masambula, Johnny Kwango, Iron Fist Clive Myers, Caswell Martin. But I was the opposite. I was considered the nasty boy. Even a lot of my own people . . . I'd bump into them in the street and they'd have a go at me.

Dave Soulman Bond: 'It started to get a little racial'

I was also known as Butcher Bond. I went in the ring, and I used to do one or two dodgy things, if I could get away with it. If the referee didn't see it, then I'd do it. But that wasn't what they expected of a black man. They expected you to be nice, and have a bit of finesse, and do the occasional cartwheel and all the rest of it. But that wasn't my type of thing – I liked to get stemmed in. There was a small minority, including the promoters, who said, We've had all the nice black guys, let's have a hard rufty-tufty black guy. They said that all the guys before me had taken a lot of stick, and now it was payback time.

My tag partner was Johnny Kincaid. We tagged as the Caribbean Sunshine Boys. That was a successful team, and I think we got a little bit too successful for the promoters. It started to get a little racial, if you like. We weren't doing any racial things in the ring, but . . . we were winning our bouts, and doing the normal gestations, the double handslaps, like gimme fives, and that sort of thing got the crowd going. At one time we had to calm down the showmanship element of it.

Max Crabtree: I split them up because they were trying to put across the race hatred. They hadn't got the formula right. It was that particular period – a lot of race hatred around, and our working-class audience felt a lot of unrest at all these people coming in from abroad.

Billy Dale said to me, 'For God's sake Max, don't let that go on.' The reaction got too wild, and wrestling's not about race relations.

Dave Soulman Bond: We've had bouts where we've had to struggle getting out of the ring because there was a National Front element in the crowd, especially in Southend. Hanley and Maidstone were also bad. In Maidstone the wrestling was in a cattle market, and there were lots and lots of gypsies. We've had full cans of Coke thrown in the ring. We literally had to bat our way back to the dressing room because fans wanted to tear us apart.

I've had incidents where I've been standing on the ring post, and someone comes up and stubs their cigarette out on your leg. You turn round to retaliate, and it's an old person, so you've got to be careful. But it wasn't just a racist thing. Big Bruno Elrington was stabbed with a knitting needle.

There was an incident where a person dragged us out of the ring. My and Johnny's photo appeared in the *Sun* under the headline 'I was bashed by tag team wrestlers'.

In the day I was working as a civil servant at the Ministry of Defence, so bloody hell. The first thing I did was go into the group captain, and told him what had happened, and he said, 'If you need a character witness I'll write it.' We had to go to court, the charge was ABH. But we got off, as we were provoked. The guy had some stitches, but he attacked us first.

Jackie Pallo Junior: The crowd always used to wind poor Johnny Kincaid up. He was very good looking, but also half-caste. He used to hit back, especially in Norwich where the farmers always used to get at him. He must have been in court half a dozen times.

Dad had to have a police escort at some places. I've been slapped and whacked and kicked and spat at. The only thing that really gets me is when I'm spat at. It's so degrading, beyond words. You can't hit back, of course, because in court you'd have no chance. Before you hit someone it's all a show, a sham. But the minute you hit someone you're a professional fighter with lethal weapon hands.

Jackie Pallo: I only ever slapped back once. I was in Doncaster when a fella in the front row kicked me hard in the ribs with the toe of his shoe. I walloped back, but he fucking moved and I hit his bird. The police came, and a nice old-school copper said, 'Jacko, I think you better go out there and apologize.' And that was it.

But the heat you could generate . . . In the ring I've looked out, and the audience members have been dead from heart attacks. I've had it twice.

Mal Sanders: It used to be that you just had to put an elbow in and they'd be booing you. Now you have to chop someone's head off to get a reaction. A piledriver used to be a finishing move. If you dropkicked someone out of the ring that would be a finish. Now all those happen in the first round, and the bloke is as right as ninepence. Modern technology.

Mal Sanders: 'We were Rock Hudsons'

8

'Eventually he went around with a sheep,' said Joe D'Orazio

Mal Sanders: I was the first person to beat McManus on television. It was an eliminator for the European title in Southport, and he cut my ear open. I beat him two falls to one and he hadn't lost on television for about twenty years. Then I beat him again two weeks later for the title in Huddersfield. Caused an uproar, and really shot me into the limelight with a catapult. That was in 1978, I was twenty. I think it was Mike Marino who came up with the name Superstar, Superstar Mal Sanders.

Then me and McManus did the rounds. At the Albert Hall I got eight stitches and lost a pint and a half of blood. He threw me out and I landed on something sharp on the apron. It hit a main artery, and it was just spurting, and a fella in the front row had a heart attack.

I was trained by Mike Marino, and became his main boy, the one that came through. He always pretended he was Italian, but he was Cockney. I used to see him every day for six years, went out to dinner a lot, and got to know his wife and daughter. He was hugely admired, ask anyone in the business. The stories he would tell – he said that gangsters used to come to his shows in the fifties. The Krays were very big fans. A lot of villains used to like the wrestling. The wrestlers were the people to be seen with.

He died on a Monday. He always used to drive to venues himself, but on this occasion he called to say could I take him, as he didn't feel up to it. So we went to Folkestone, and he didn't look well. He was always laughing and joking, but he was very quiet. He was going to wrestle Big Jim Harris, a big coloured fella. Peter Szakacs just said, 'Well do what you can,' but I said there was no way he could wrestle, he looked awful.

Joe D'Orazio: I was booked to referee at Leas Cliff Hall, Folkestone and one of the contestants was reigning British mid-heavyweight champion Mike Marino, my cousin. As soon as he walked into the dressing room it was obvious that something was wrong with him. He was sweating profusely, and his normal suntanned face was almost grey.

'I've got to go on. My name's on the bill and I'm here. I can't let the public down.'

We spent the best part of an hour trying to talk him out of it. He even started putting his boots on until I told him that if he got in the ring he'd be in there on his own as I wouldn't referee. Finally he agreed to step into the ring just to show faith with the audience, and as the first match got underway he went back to the dressing room.

Mal Sanders: Mike went off to Ashford Hospital, I wrestled and when I got there I expected to find him all tucked up in bed with the doctors round him. But he was sitting in the waiting room. He had a towel up to his mouth – what had happened was his tongue had swollen up, and they had given him an injection to take it down. He had trouble speaking, and all he could say was, 'I want to go home.' I found out later that they wanted to keep him in, but he signed himself out.

We got about twenty or thirty miles down the road and he started having what I thought was a convulsive fit. He had swallowed his tongue and couldn't breathe. I stopped the car, pitch black, not a lit-up area on that part of the M20. His tongue came loose and after about a minute he was telling me that he was going to die. I dragged him out the car. I was only eleven stone then, and Mike was fifteen. I lent him up against the crash barrier and all he could say to me was that he was going to die. I was trying to open his mouth and do everything I could for him, but his jaw was locked. I had a screwdriver with me, and thought about doing one of those tracheotomies, jamming it into his throat, but then I thought, What if it goes wrong? What if I kill him? But then I felt for his pulse and knew that he was already dead.

I thought to myself, How can a fella who has given so many people so much enjoyment throughout his life just die on the side of a road? I hailed a man who'd just come off the ferry on his holidays, and his wife went to call the ambulance. The ambulancemen were wrestling people and recognized us immediately. They put the electric shock paddles on, but it had been fifteen minutes by then.

It turned out later Mike actually had leukaemia. They said he had the heart of a twenty-year-old.

That was 1981. The big talk of the wrestling business – a catastrophe. The next day I was with a guy called Billy Torontos, and Billy said to me, 'I'll be the next one to go. Not many old ones left now.' A month to the day Billy Torontos died. Wrestled at Peterborough, up to the dressing room, heart attack.

Mike Marino:
All he could say was,
'I want to go home'

Big Jim Harris, the Mississippi Mauler: Billy was in a very thoughtful mood that day. We listened to the midday news together over a cup of coffee and it was the usual sort of thing – trouble in Ireland, trouble in the Middle East, Russia accusing America, the USA accusing Russia. I think the last thing I heard Billy say before he went out was that the world was in a terrible state and that all that was needed to put

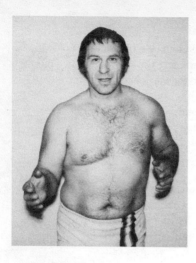

Billy Torontos:
'He always spoke to me'

things right was for everyone to try to love each other.

The doorbell rang about this time. It was lightweight champion Steve Grey calling to ask if Billy wanted a lift to Peterborough.

Joe D'Orazio: 'Ladies and gentlemen,' John Curry, the MC said, 'in round six, the winner by two falls to one, the Chicago Express . . . Billy Torontos!'

Billy did his usual half-dozen laps of victory, running round the ring with one arm held high.

Billy was an amazing man. He wanted to be like Milo of Croton, the ancient Greek. He imitated that thing he did with the bullock. Milo got this one-day-old bullock across his shoulders and walked around the arena with it, then did the same thing when the bullock was two days, then three days, until at last he could walk around the arena with a fully grown bullock on his shoulders. Now this may have just been a load of bullock. Billy couldn't get his hands on a bullock, but he used to mind his dad's sheep in the hills, and so he did it with a baby lamb, then a week-old lamb, then a month-old and eventually he went around with a sheep.

On that fateful night he walked back to his dressing room where some of the other wrestlers were waiting to congratulate him.

'Good match, Billy,' said Big Daddy.

'Terrific,' said Steve Grey.

82

Steve Grey: I thought he was kidding . . . he made that funny noise he used to make when he was going to town in the ring and then he just seemed to topple over sideways with his cigar butt still in his hand.

Joe D'Orazio: Within the hour, news of Billy's death was being broadcast on the local radio station. Two weeks later an elderly lady told me with tears in her eyes, 'I always go to see Billy wrestle at the Wirrina Stadium, and I had only returned home a few minutes. I put the kettle on and switched on the radio. I just couldn't believe it . . . I still can't believe it. He always spoke to me.'

Alan Strongman Dennison told me, 'If ever a man was loved by one and all, it was Billy Tornado Torontos. He only had to show his face in a dressing room to make everyone except his opponent happy.'

I saw Big Daddy a few days later. 'You know, Joe,' he said, 'I'm sure that Billy died in my arms that night. I keep thinking about it all the time. I thought of nothing else all the way back to Yorkshire that night.'

Mal Sanders: A couple of months later I was wrestling at the Dome in Brighton, and a message comes that there's a lady and a young girl who would like to see me in the bar. We used to have a lot of messages from girls who wanted to buy you drinks. So I went upstairs and met them, and this woman says, 'I've got a message for you.' I say, 'Who's it from?' She says, 'Mike Marino.'

I told her Mike was dead, and she said that she knew, and that he was very sorry for what happened, and that in a previous life I had actually died in his arms. I thought, 'Oh, she's one of those cranks.'

But we kept on talking, and she was telling me things that happened that she couldn't have possibly known, things that I had forgotten about. It was as if she was there watching the whole proceedings, how I lent him up against the barriers, about how I was thinking about the screwdriver. The girl with her said that she was one of the top mediums, in those days when all you knew was Doris Stokes and Doris Collins. The woman asked me to a séance next week to get in touch with him, but I didn't go. Too strange.

Alan Dennison:
'The secret of staying young was to train with young men'

Later they had a contest for the Mike Marino Memorial Shield, which I was lucky enough to win. His wife Renee presented it. As she came in to give it to me I said 'My God Reen, you're looking well.' And she said, 'You lying bastard!'

Max Crabtree: Alan Dennison didn't smoke or drink. If anything he had a hangup about staying young. Alan was the chap who, when we were driving down overnight from Scotland, he'd stay awake all night chatting with me at the wheel. We'd get back at eight in the morning, probably a horrible wet day, and whereas most would just crawl under the covers he went straight to the gym, to lift iron, not chrome. He'd been giving me a theory on life: he told me the secret of staying young was to train with young men, do the same weights they did.

The day he died he had a heavy workout, and I think he over-taxed his heart. He was wrestling at the Floral Hall, Southport, a hot night. I was the MC that evening. After the fight I went into his dressing room to say hello, and he had his head bent down. I thought he was winded. I said, 'Are you all right, Alan?' but sadly he'd gone into convulsions and was in the last stage of dying. I couldn't believe it – still had his arm bands on, all his gear. I laid him on his side. Shirley went to get the manager and ambulance, but by the time they arrived poor Alan had a massive heart attack and died. I went to the hospital at Southport, and from behind a screen all I could see sticking out was a pair of wrestling boots. I thought how ironic: one minute they were cheering their heads off for him, and there he was, lying dead.

9

'Could you do me a favour?' asked Esther Rantzen

Jackie Pallo: 'When I walk into a gents' toilet, everyone turns around and looks'

Kent Walton: Most folks have no idea. People say, 'Oh people don't get hurt, it's all acting,' but I can give them fifteen names of people who died in the last six years. They died just after a wrestling bout. Is that fixed?

People say, 'Ah yes, but you can't say that just because wrestlers die, that proves it's not fixed.' But what more proof do they want? These fellas are dead! Gone!

News of the World, 27 February 1972:

FAKED! And We Show You How It's Done

Millions of television viewers thrilled to this professional wrestling bout last week. They saw Albert 'Rocky' Wall, billed as British and Commonwealth heavyweight champion, draw with 'British mid-heavyweight champion' Mike Marino.

The entire bout, we can report, was planned in advance. In other words, faked.

Hidden microphones at the New Victoria Hall, Halifax, Yorks, revealed the detailed dressing room rehearsal for the 'fight' last Wednesday.

The whole thing was recorded on tape by the *News of the World*'s famous special investigation team as part of a nationwide probe into the wrestling business. A transcript of the tape-recordings shows these exchanges:

WALL: What are we doing Michael? You get the first fall, I get a submission . . .

MARINO: Which way do you want to come at it? Across the ring?

The wrestlers then practise the lead-up to Marino's fall, a leg snatch and folding press in Round 3, and the planning moves on to the equalising submission.

WALL: The arm job, eh? Simple as that. The ordinary arm job lift-up one . . . Then we do the head-butt. You get two or three near falls . . . Out of the blue I'll give you that head-butt again . . . I'm groggy . . . I pick you up. I fall into the ropes so the ref will break it up, so I whack you.

And that, as anyone who saw the bout will tell you, is EXACTLY what happened.

The action sent TV commentator Kent Walton into descriptive

ecstasies. 'There's no doubt about it, we've really got two experts in the ring . . . Wall occasionally goes a little beserk, specially when he's up against a master wrestler like he is now . . . It's really a question of whether Marino can last out with his left arm in as much trouble as it is.'

Jackie Pallo's Autobiography, *You Grunt, I'll Groan*: Wrestling is a branch of showbusiness. How desperate we all were to protect the name of our game, the image, the great illusion, the belief of several million faithful fans that professional wrestling is a straight, competitive sport in which the best man wins. All nonsense of course, but everybody in the game is brainwashed into believing that it will die if the punters ever suspect that it is all a fake.

Pallo's book: 'How desperate we all were to protect the name of our game'

Ideally, every bout should tell a little tale. Perhaps I would build up a story around my opponent's left arm, which would be heavily bandaged at the elbow. I'd keep attacking it, jerking it hard, then jeer at him and the punters. 'He's working on that weak arm again,' Kent Walton would say sadly. 'I don't now how much more of that Bert Royal can take.' Any amount: it wasn't hurting him nearly as much as he pretended.

Normally I like to wrestle straight for a short while from the off, letting my opponent make the moves. Then I'd start to take over and, maybe, get him to the deck and stand over him so he couldn't get up. That always gees up the crowd. Or perhaps I'd drag him off the floor, which is 'illegal', throw him about a bit, use the elbow, and be generally dastardly. Then, just as it looked as if it was all over for him, he'd make a comeback and I'd be in all sorts of trouble.

'Take me leg, throw me off the ropes, chin me,' I'd whisper. The crowd loved it, and as soon as they were up, ranting, I'd mutter, 'Die again, die. Leave it to me. Bring 'em down,' and you could almost hear the punters collectively groaning, 'Gawd, the bastard's got him again.'

If I was about to start on a series of fights with another good pro, I'd just get together with him and we'd discuss how to play it. I'd say something like, 'Right, I'll take a fall in the second, you take one in the fourth, and I'll finish with my usual back submission in the fifth.'

Outsiders were never allowed in the dressing room. If some geezer walked in unexpectedly, a voice would say, 'Queens, queens,' and everybody would stop talking. Queens was short for Queens Park Rangers, which in Cockney rhyming slang means strangers.

Simon Garfield: The first time I saw Pallo outside the ring was one blazing August afternoon when he picked me up at Ramsgate train station to drive me to his house. We shook hands at the ticket barrier and he hobbled back in his small shorts and T-shirt and flip flops to his old Saab 900. I told him I had an old Saab too. He said, 'Simon, I have *lots* of Saabs.'

He said he moved down to Kent fourteen years ago from Totteridge when he had an offer on his place he just couldn't refuse – crazy money.

We arrived at his house, and parked in deep overgrowth. Around us there were eight or nine other Saabs, various old models, 900s, 99s and 96s, all rusting away, not buffed like most collectors'. He said he doesn't like the new models since General Motors took over.

His son was in the garden, wearing even shorter shorts, nothing else, lazing on his back. In the distance some goats chewed grass and plants. There was a huge rectangular hole at the bottom of the garden: they were building themselves a swimming pool. 'Should have had it finished by now,' Pallo said, 'but I've been unwell with flu and we've missed the summer altogether. There's still something nasty on my lungs they're trying to sort out. Also, we got the wrong bloody tiles.'

'He's all right,' he said, introducing me to his son. 'He's a Saab man.'

Jackie Pallo Junior ('JJ') looked me over through his sunglasses. Senior fetched some beers from his wife Trixie in the kitchen, and we sat round a table. Senior took off his T-shirt, to reveal the text-book definition of out of shape.

Jackie Pallo: When the book came out some were angry because I'd earned money.

Jackie Pallo Junior: One was upset because his name was spelt wrong.

Jackie Pallo: One bloke got upset. I said, 'Leave off, you're talking to Jack here. I've been around a long time. I could take your arm off and stick it up your arse. I was born in the East End, I'm a hard fella. But I spoke the truth, and I never knocked a wrestler. I never would.

Jackie Pallo Junior: People think we rehearsed the throws in the gym or backstage, but we never did. We ad-libbed it. We were pros. It's not supposed to be by numbers. It should flow, be spontaneous, and you should adapt to the audience. It's a show, but it's not 100 per cent scripted and rehearsed. Even the falls can be ad-libbed. It depends on the wrestler and on the promoter. Occasionally wrestlers get out of hand and just sort it out by themselves in the ring. Either the wrestlers or the promoters sort out the falls. With wrestling the lovely thing is we just suspend reality. It's like *Star Trek*. People come to the wrestling to be entertained. That's what we're doing, entertaining. That's all.

Jackie Pallo: It's like a comedian standing on stage, he gets a kick when he gets laughs. I got a kick when I got booed. It was nice in those days to think that people came just to boo you.

Max Crabtree: When people say it's a well-rehearsed script . . . bollocks. Most guys haven't got the intelligence to do a well-rehearsed script.

Them that like us, they can write what the hell they want. If they like wrestling, no explanation is needed of how wrestling works. Those that don't like us, any explanation about it is not good enough. Jackie's book didn't have any real impact on the business. We've had many exposés, and it's all come from within, out of jealousy mostly. Don Branch gave the newspapers some stuff. I'm not pretending that pro-wrestling is an Olympic Games sport. It's full of razzmatazz, but it's a tough business and it always was. To do it right.

Robbie Brookside: At the least possible chance Pallo tries to drag this business through the gutter. And he got so much money out of it. In the sixties it was reputed that Pallo earned the average man's weekly wage every night. So seven days a week he would earn about £20 a night – today that would be like £300 a night. But have you ever seen Pallo wrestle? There's something wrong somewhere.

Brian Dixon: What do journalists mean when they say it's all fixed? They've never really thought about it. How could it all be fixed? If you throw somebody into a post, how is that fixed? People get mistaken between fixed and showbiz . . . It's the same with footballers – they want characters. And when people say about wrestling, 'Oh, the pain's not as bad as they make out,' they never say that about football, do they? People writhing on the ground, wriggling in pain. You're not going to tell me that that writhing's not fixed?

Don Branch: At sixteen I was amateur lightweight champion of Yorkshire. Between 1948 and 1951 I represented England and in 1949 I became middleweight champion of northern England. In other words, I was a real wrestler.

Within a few days of turning pro I realized what play-acting professional wrestling is. In my second bout, at Halifax, I fought the British lightweight champion Johnny Stead. To this day I can remember him saying to me in the third round, 'Right, get your fall now,' and me pinning him.

They used to write the instructions on a slip of paper in those days, but this was stopped after two of these 'scripts' got into the wrong hands.

I was nominated, purely for publicity purposes of course, as wrestler of the year. Next year I was made the 'winner' of a fifteen-man tournament in Newcastle-upon-Tyne. I quote 'winner' because the action and the results of all the bouts were carefully worked out in the promoters' office during the day. Equally a charade are the various championship titles held by wrestlers.

After thirteen years, I turned referee. I discovered I had to be as good an actor as before. Once at Bradford I was refereeing a bout featuring Alan Dennison. My orders were to disqualify him in about round five. Dennison promptly gave me a forearm smash. MC Ernest Lofthouse whispered, 'Whack him, then challenge him.' I fought Dennison two weeks later and won – arranged so my authority as a ref remained intact.

Pat Roach: Whatever you write about wrestling, about the theatre side of it, I would never try to insult your intelligence about the question of was it real or was it fixed. We won't go into those realms. I would have thought we both respect each other's integrity far more than to discuss things like that.

But . . . all the wrestlers were thrown together in one vehicle. Anywhere else in the world the heels would travel in one car, and the nice guys would go in another. That was the very least they could do.

Kent Walton: I used to say to people who thought it was all fixed that I'd give them £100 if they got into the ring with a wrestler of my choice who would be at least one stone lighter. No one ever took me up on that. The promoters didn't like it, because they knew that the tough boys like Kellett would break somebody's back.

Pat Roach: 'The public wouldn't buy him'

Max Crabtree: Did you ever see that programme *Big Time*, with Esther Rantzen? About this man who wanted to become a professional wrestler. It was the same year she did Sheena Easton. I trained this man called Keith Rawlinson, a schoolteacher from Burnley who played organ at the church on Sundays, a big wrestling fan. We called him Rip Rawlinson. We trained him for six months, but he was just the wrong shape.

Eventually we put this Keith Rawlinson in at the Albert Hall with John Naylor, a wrestler from Wigan. Esther chose John herself from photos we gave her because she thought he looked angelic and not too big. Unfortunately Wigan wrestlers have a reputation for breaking people's legs.

I told John to go easy on him, but he just annihilated him. John didn't give him anything, poor lad, wouldn't let him have a drink of water. So he threw him all over and dropped him on his head. After seven minutes John got so bored that he decided to finish it with a submission hold – he trapped his leg up his back, stepped over his other leg, sat back and put a face bar on.

The schoolteacher was in such excruciating agony that he couldn't even say 'I submit', so the hold was held on. After a few seconds the referee realized he was almost dying, so he broke the hold. The poor man went straight to hospital on a stretcher and stayed in overnight.

Mal Sanders: I met Keith Rawlinson at Leicester. He said, 'When I watch it on TV, that is me in there . . .' He absolutely refused to believe that there was any showmanship in the job.

Max Crabtree: A couple of days later the phone rings in my office and it's Esther. She says, 'Max, I wonder if you could do me a favour.' Esther didn't want the programme to end with him in hospital of course, so they ignored that bit and she called me up and said would I mind, a few days later, going down to meet him at the Albert Hall stage door so it looked like he was just leaving with his kitbag after the match. I was happy to do that. Esther was so thrilled with the film.

Mal Sanders: Well it's not choreographed like people think – how can you work out a twenty-minute fight with someone when you only get to the venue at seven-thirty and you're on at eight? It's just that people know what they're doing. There are times when it gets out of hand and you are doing it for real. It's not all like *Come Dancing*.

Peter Blake: I saw three McManus–Pallo fights at the Albert Hall. The one I remember was the third one. They'd won one each, and I think the third one was a genuine fight to the finish. They came out, and McManus went straight over, without any holds or anything, and nutted Pallo on the forehead. That's all he did, the whole fight he just kept nutting him. Eventually Pallo realized he couldn't go on. For a while he thought, 'We'll get through this and carry on,' but then he realized that his whole forehead was split open and there was blood in his eyes and he couldn't see. It was just a cynical taking out. McManus just decided that was how he would do it. It was a street-fight, and Pallo realized too late what had been done to him.

Simon Garfield: The blood was real, but its production was often pre-planned. Wrestlers liked to produce 'the claret' by nicking themselves or an opponent with a sliver of razor blade taped to a finger. The blade would then be disposed of by the referee. Occasionally the referee might do the cutting himself, slicing an earlobe while bending over to examine an 'injury'. Jackie Pallo preferred to bite his own lip. He said the blade made him nervous.

Peter Blake: There had to be a morality, a code, a guide to what you couldn't do. But occasionally that morality was broken. I often saw holds on legs where one wrestler went too far, and put a leg out of action. That could happen at any time, but you rarely saw it. I saw it perhaps three times. Once I saw Tony St Clair fall to the ground shouting, 'I can't see, I've gone blind.' Something had happened – his eyes had been poked. His terror was genuine. You'd know instantly that a leg was broken or that someone was in genuine pain.

Things changed. In the early days the Boston crab was always a submission hold, without fail. Once they were in a Boston crab you knew it was the end of the fight. But later they could always get out of the Boston crab. I don't know what happened.

The Times, 26 June 1981: The night Masambula, the wrestler, appeared at Preston Guildhall, it was agreed that he was to lose to Peter Roberts, his opponent, by feigning injury in the fourth round.

But the bout did not go beyond the third round because Masambula suffered a genuine back injury which ended his career as a professional wrestler, Mr Geoffrey Rivlin, QC, his counsel, said, opening a claim for damages in the High Court at Leeds yesterday.

Masambula – real name Mr Mam Buna Jeng – aged 57, sued wrestling promoters Morrell and Beresford Ltd, and Mr Billy Shinfield, the erector of the ring at Preston on 19 February 1975. Both denied liability.

Mr Rivlin said that before the bout Mr Ernest Lofthouse, the master of ceremonies, said Mr Roberts was to win in the fourth round, and Masambula was to feign injury.

Masambula was injured when he was propelled backwards against one of the corner posts. The ropes of the ring were far too slack to provide adequate protection, and there was a centre bolt hook which did not recede on impact.

Daily Mail, 26 June 1981: On a specially installed TV, Mr Justice Skinner spent nearly an hour watching a video recording of the fight. He saw the 13 stone 6lb wrestler, wearing a leopardskin cloak and head-dress, being cheered into the ring and described as 'the man himself' by commentator Kent Walton.

The Times, 1 July 1981: Masambula, the wrestler, yesterday won his court action against a firm of match promoters and a ring constructor for a back injury he received during a fight.

He was awarded £20,710 damages. After the hearing, Masambula said, 'I have proved my point, but I am still the loser. I can never wrestle again, my love life is ruined, and the wrestling world has turned its back on me.'

Last night he would not elaborate about fight rigging. 'If the public knew what really went on it would ruin their enjoyment of the game.'

Masambula, once the favourite wrestler of many housewives, now lives on social security at Buttershaw, Bradford, West Yorkshire.

*

Pallo performs his
Boston crab

Jackie Pallo Junior: I grew up in it, wrestling with Dad in the front room since I was eight. I saw my dad get hurt. I kicked Mick once because he'd hurt Dad.

If you're naturally exhibitionist there are only a few things you can do: you can't go and be a bank clerk. So I went into the theatre for four years. I started off as a dresser for Brian Rix in the West End. Him and Leslie Crowther taught me an awful lot. But wrestling still had this allure.

I started when I was sixteen, in Shrewsbury. Absolutely petrified. I could barely walk to the ring. I laced my boot up before I went in, but realized I'd forgotten to put my foot in it. In my first year I broke my collar-bone, dislocated my knee, ripped my cartilage. I broke my collar-bone just doing a forward roll. I collapsed in the corner like a jelly, and everyone either laughed or booed, because it looked absolute shit. They all thought I was faking it.

Max Crabtree: Jackie had a lovely bungalow in Barnet, nice swimming pool, and he'd change his Saab every year. He'd done well with Dale Martin. There's no fortunes in wrestling for anybody. I must point that out. There never has been, and there never will be. Wrestling is a very working-class sport or entertainment. It's the people's sport.

Jackie went out and tried to promote by himself. At that time I was his rabbi. He'd ring me as many as five or six times a day. He was going through a terrible stage. Of course I doubt if he'd ever even considered that you can lose money promoting. He always had his wage packet, irrelevant of whether anyone was in or not. All of a sudden when you put your own money down . . . Poor old Jack ended up . . . he got himself so involved. His lad didn't help, because he was full of it. He thought his dad were the bee's knees, which can only be right. But he should have tried to help his dad and say, 'Look Dad, please don't throw away all that hard-earned money.'

He tried to oppose the other promoters, and they closed ranks on him. Which is understandable – that's how business is run. If you step on their territory, they're going to use the powers they've got.

Mick McManus: When Pallo stopped fighting he thought he knew everything about the game, and thought he'd set up promoting on his own. But he lost a lot of money. He was a terrible businessman. But I don't mean that in a derogatory way: he was just bad at business. One friend I'd talked to said he'd turn up to appear on a Pallo bill and there were supposed to be ten people there, and often there were only seven. But sometimes there were twelve. He says he's got all these other things going now, but I'm not sure. Reg Gutteridge, the boxing commentator, is a friend of mine, and he's Pallo's cousin. That's Pallo's real name – Jackie Gutteridge.

Pat Roach: Pallo is absolutely bitter. If you get your living from a business for all those years and then you squeal on it like a shit-house rat, and then you decide to come back into it again, then what do you expect? You're going to be squeezed out. Because of wrestling he earnt good money. He went into pantomime and should have got good dough. The couple of pantomimes I've done were very lucrative. They drive you barmy, though.

I did this *Pebble Mill* TV programme with him when he defended his book and all the other wrestlers were against him. He admitted to being in bent matches himself but he didn't say everyone else's were. At the end of it he did a song and dance routine, 'I'll Never Have Another Cigarette'. I'll always respect Pallo for his gameness.

Jackie Pallo: I tried to get my own fights on TV, but Joint Promotions had been there for twenty years. Couldn't get rid of them. In the end we had everybody on our books – Adrian Street, Les Kellett, everybody. They left Joint Promotions because it was being run by idiots. Whereas before it was being run by wrestlers. Jack Dale was a *wrestler*. All the others came into the business afterwards.

Max Crabtree said I should have got out with him five years before I did. We ran a big show on Clapham Common, and Dale Martin offered him a job and took him away. He done what he thought was best for himself, which is right – you do. But I didn't: I worried about wrestlers. And doing that fucked myself. The wrestling business was a fabulous business ruined by greed. Greed.

When I went out on my own, one promoter took me to dinner and said, 'Jackie I wish you all the luck in the world to get on in showbusiness, but we're going to destroy you as a promoter.' I said, 'Well, buy me out.' He said, 'No, we'll destroy you.'

10

'My dress – ruined!' said Klondyke Kate

Klondyke Kate:
'I know how to
work the crowd'

Pat Roach: British wrestling was sold to thirty-seven outlets throughout the world. I saw a list I wasn't supposed to see, from a friend who worked on television. I imagine that the amount of money generated was amazing, but the promoters put absolutely nothing back: the thought of spending £100 on a new ring would have horrified them, so some of the rings were in a dreadful state, falling apart, with no padding, just bare boards and concrete all around. The ring at the Albert Hall was one of the worst in the country, and even though we packed the venue, they never had the best matches because there was no way I was going to hoist a very well-respected opponent up above my head and slam him into that hard mat. What for? That man has to learn a living too. I wouldn't take the risks. You never got the same show out of me at a hard ring as you did at a decent ring.

I've always been big, but not so heavy. But I trained heavy all my life, so I put that weight on over the years. I was never a weight lifter, and I'm still not a good one at all. But I trained with weights, and respect weights, and I think weights have a place in everyone's life.

I never had a gimmick. I remember being asked by a reporter twenty years ago whether I had a gimmick, and I said Yes, and he expected me to say I have a balloon on a stick and a feather up my arse, or something. But I said, 'My gimmick is that I'm six foot five or six foot six inches tall, I'm nineteen or twenty stone, I'm in good condition and I can wrestle.'

Today big men are plentiful, because what's happening now is that people are taking all sorts of drugs. But natural big men used to be a rarity. I was a giant at . . . well, I've only ever been six foot four and a half inches in my life, but the truth is we all tell lies about our height. I never have, funnily enough, not because I'm honest, but because other people have done it for me. Some people wouldn't have me anything less than six foot six.

I admired the wrestlers I saw when I was growing up, wanted to become one of them and I did. I excelled at the profession. Not only that, but it supplied me with a stepping stone into the film industry.

Over here I only went on television after I'd already established myself in the film industry, after *Auf Wiedersehen Pet*. Nowadays

I sign three different types of autographs – wrestling autographs, *Auf Wiedersehen Pet* autographs and then all the other movie autographs. I did *Prince of Thieves* and *Indiana Jones III*, but in both of those I finished up on the cutting room floor. Very sad, because those two movies could have shot me into really really serious stuff. In *Indiana Jones* I was dressed as a giant Adolf Hitler. Spielberg told me that he saw me wrestle in Los Angeles before he became famous. He was a fan. I was also in *Barry Lyndon* and *A Clockwork Orange*. I worked with Olivier as well. I played two parts in *Conan the Destroyer*.

Brian Crabtree: What really put him up front was *Auf Wiedersehen Pet*, and we thought it would be great if he came into the ring accompanied by the theme tune. But no, he wanted to enter like John the Baptist. He had a dressing gown down to his ankles and he came in to this heavy music.

Pat Roach: On *Indiana II*, Spielberg contacted me and asked if I would train him and Harrison Ford. I was very surprised. I knew Harrison quite well by now – he'd killed me four times – and he wasn't the training type. But I said I didn't want to be known as a trainer, I wanted to be known as an actor. But I did set them up at Borehamwood with some equipment, and they imported a trainer called Jake from LA.

I've had the chance to go over and live in Hollywood many times, but I've always said no. Must have been mad, but I love this dirty old town Birmingham. I love the people, and I feel I belong to every single one of them.

Max Crabtree: Pat's wrestling abilities were good – six foot six, in very good order, but he had no direction. The public wouldn't buy him. There were many promoters who thought they had a catch when they booked Pat, but sadly when they looked at the takings they'd lost money. And sometimes we'd be stood in the foyer talking, and a spectator would come along and say, 'Excuse me, Pat, can I have your autograph?' And Pat wouldn't speak to him, but keep talking to me. I'd say, 'Pat, can you sign this autograph for this chap?' Pat would say, 'I don't sign anything. What were you saying, Max?'

Pat Roach: The unfortunate thing for me was that my face never fitted with promoters. I buggered off abroad with Johnny Kowalski and Klondyke Jake. Abroad we became international wrestlers of note.

I had a reputation for not turning up, but God knows where I got that from. Just like the rest of them I could get the flu and get injured. But nothing to do with bad timekeeping or unprofessionalism. I wrestled for four years without going on television. They had no interest in putting me on. The promoters felt that if they put us on television we'd then bugger off abroad, and they wouldn't be able to exploit us in the coming weeks and months. If you accepted work elsewhere you were fired.

Once I got fired because I told a joke in the dressing room. I'd just got back from abroad, and Mick McManus and [the promoter] Mike Judd were in the dressing room with some other lads. Mick had the power of the pen at Dale Martin's at that time, deciding who went on and with whom.

I said I'd heard about this bird who got married three times and never got fucked. The first time she married a French guy who wasn't too fussy on actual intercourse, he was a bit of an oral man. So she didn't get on too well with that guy, so she got divorced and married a Greek guy. Now he too had his peculiarities. He also didn't like to do actual intercourse, he liked to do it backwards with her. It has been generally known that Greeks do it that way. She didn't like that too much, so she got rid of him. Then she married an Englishman. She thought, I can't go wrong with an Englishman – they're not too perverted. They're known as being a bit cold if anything, but certainly they like to fuck. So she married an Englishman, but it turned out to be an English wrestling promoter. And sure enough, once again she never got fucked, because he was too busy screwing his boys. So I told that joke, meaning he was screwing them financially. McManus and Judd scowled. Then next day I got the sack.

Brian Dixon: Dale Martin's and Joint Promotions made it very easy for me. They were so blasé. They had a stranglehold, but they didn't look after it.

I'd always been a fan. I went to the Liverpool Stadium every

Friday, started writing for the weekly programme, ran a fan club magazine for Cry Baby Jim Breaks. I did something called the *Wrestler's A–Z*. From then it was seconding in the corner, getting to know the local wrestlers, hanging out at the gym and then moving into refereeing.

My father feared the wrestling was taking over, and I was persuaded to get a job, first as a relief manager of a grocery firm, then as a salesman selling cooked meats and sausages. I got Salesman of the Year, with my cooked meats. The job allowed me to watch wrestling all over the country, and often I'd plan my routes according to the most attractive bouts.

In the early seventies I was refereeing a bout with Mitzi Mueller, and there was a bit of a thing because I trod on her hair in the ring. An accident. She said she was finding it hard to get fights because many promoters thought women's wrestling wasn't right and they had doubts about her abilities. I began promoting her, and then going out with her.

Before the first show I was threatened by another promoter, 'If you run that show, you'll regret it.' It went ahead at Marple Baths outside Manchester, I got away unharmed with £150. I spent the night at Mitzi's, and woke up to find that my takings had been stolen from my car. I thought, 'This is a challenge.'

She was known before, but soon things started to get very successful. I began to promote bills around her – three male bouts and one female. My ladies were getting great publicity. I had Hellcat Haggerty, Naughty Nancy Barton, Lolita Loren and the Cassidy girls. Most wrestlers you find have family connections. Jack Cassidy had four daughters, so there was a ready-made family of wrestlers right away. Roy Bull Davis, Skull Murphy's father, an old-time sixties heavyweight, he married a woman and brought her daughter into it. Mitzi's real name was Connolly. Local councils invariably kicked up a big fuss wherever they went, and they were banned entirely in London. But fans were grateful when the women came to town – something they hadn't seen before.

Max Crabtree: I never promoted them. I'm a male chauvinist pig. Listen, when the Boxing Board of Control gives licences to women to box, then maybe I might change my mind. But no. It's strictly a man's game. I've been married for forty years. Do you think that for my work I want to take bloody women round the country? You put two women in a dressing room and you know what the end result is. No, no, they're better in the kitchen.

Mitzi Mueller: My father was a wrestler, in his day a big name, and he used to take me down to the gym in Manchester and show me a few moves. My mother wouldn't let me go and watch him – thought it was too frightening. He retired not long after I was born. I think he made a promise to my mum.

I just thought I'd like to become a lady wrestler. My school gym instructor said, 'Good on you!'

There was very little women's wrestling when I started. It wasn't easy, no special treatment. I used to travel in the ring van, and put the ring up before the show and then take it down again. My mother had a German name, so I took that. There was already an American wrestler, a big name, she was the Fabulous Moolah. I just thought Mitzi Mueller was catchy. I prefer it when people call me by my wrestling name now.

My first bout was with Naughty Nancy Barton. I think it lasted three rounds. She got me in an aeroplane spin, and instead of throwing me down so that I'd land on my feet, she threw me out so that I landed on my face, and knocked me out. I thought, 'Right girl, you're not ready for this yet. More training.' I was fourteen, skinny really.

I trained with men, and did all the regular moves. They weren't gentle with you, which made me glad. There were quite a few who didn't want to train with me, thought women wrestlers shouldn't be allowed. Some people, maybe those who never saw me, thought it must be an erotic thing, but I never saw it like that. There probably were the mac brigade. But I never ever had anyone come up to me. I was a good girl in the ring, I think because I could actually wrestle and didn't have to rely on dirty antics. Whether it was my blond hair or not I don't know, but people instantly took to me.

I first saw Brian in Wales when he refereed me. I used to have very very long hair then, and I'd just got a fall on my opponent. I tried to get up, and he was stood on my hair and I pulled a lot of my hair out. Afterwards I saw him in the dressing room and said,

'If you do ever referee again, keep your bloody feet out the way.' Twenty-seven years ago.

At the beginning I was wrestling four or five times a week, and then doing television work. Even people who have never been to a wrestling show, somewhere along the line they have heard the name Mitzi Mueller. I used to have a fantastic following, especially at places like the Liverpool Stadium. Young kids . . . I worked hard for them and they worked hard for me. Television didn't make me – it was pure hard work slogging around. I would never refuse an autograph. I always had time for my fans. I saw a banner once – Mitzi Walks On Water. So many people came up and said, 'Would you mind if I called my daughter after you, or my cat or my dog?' No problem whatsoever.

When I did *Emmerdale* I was an exotic dancer. I played a Russian sea officer in *Minder*. *Juliet Bravo*, so many. Pantomime. The play *Trafford Tanzi* was written about me. Claire Luckham was in honeymoon in Paignton, and they came to the show, and from that she went on to write the play. The very first production of that I trained the actresses, and then many productions afterwards. At first I thought it couldn't be done, to learn those moves in only a couple of weeks. It was the same every night, but they still had to take the bumps and fly off the top rope.

I think I can partly take the credit for the expansion in ladies' wrestling. I was wrestling with Loretta Loren, Hellcat Haggerty, Jodie Lees. I don't keep in touch. I wouldn't have called any of them friends. They'd be nice to your face, but behind your back they'd stab you. Jealousy.

When I first wrestled Klondyke Kate she imagined me as an old woman, because she'd heard the name so often. I first wrestled her in Blackpool, and she was crying because she was that nervous at going on with me.

Max Crabtree: Mitzi is a nice enough lass, I don't dislike her. But they came in on the back of the popularity of the wrestling that was on television. Klondyke Kate . . . she was one of my customers – Jane Porter. She came to Victoria Hall, Hanley, when she was a young girl about ten or eleven, and she came for many years. I remember she went to Blackpool for a September break and she

Mitzi Mueller: 'I always
had time for my fans'

loved it. She came back and said, 'I'm wrestling now.' But no matter who they were, and I say this respectfully, there was never ever a place for them in the history of British wrestling. I think that if I had attempted to put them on television, ITV would have instantly taken it off.

Klondyke Kate: I went to Blackpool to watch a show when I was fifteen. I saw Mighty Chang, a big tall bald-headed man who petrified me. I had this long white dress on, a special occasion dress. Mighty Chang was bleeding and fell out of the ring, and I was in the front row and his blood went all over me. All over my white dress and my sandals. I thought, 'I'm not having this.'

I went to see the promoter and said, 'My dress – ruined! I can't be doing with this.' He chatted away, and started talking about wrestling, and I forgot about my dress after a while. This was

Robby Baron. I told him I was interested in wrestling, and he said he'd give me a try if I wanted. I thought, It's very hard getting into wrestling – I can't see how this is so easy. I thought it would be impossible to get in.

I'm thirty-three now. I was born in Stoke-on-Trent, into a family of pottery workers. I used to go to the wrestling at the local hall with my grandmother, one of the handbag brigade. She was totally obsessed with it, lived for Saturday afternoon.

In those days I didn't know there were women wrestlers. I saw people like the Royal Brothers, Billy Howes. You only had to look at Billy Howes to hate him, which I thought was fantastic. Count Bartelli, Mick McManus. I liked Jon Cortez, who did absolutely nothing in the ring but could just wind people up by looking at them. People used to be tearing their hair out as he climbed in, well before he made any moves. I thought it was wonderful.

My hero was Steve Logan. He would look at people and they would melt, petrified. He used to put the fear of God into people and now he's a little old man, and a bit forgetful and he can't walk too well. I met him and he gave me a marvellous compliment. His actual words were, 'You can backdrop me any day,' which was the best thing he could have said because it means he likes what you're doing.

The first girls I saw were very beautiful, Rusty Blair from Scotland with fiery red hair, and the Cherokee Princess – the head-dress, all the business and lovely figures. I thought, Oh my God, there *are* girls, but they're all very pretty. I wasn't that big when I was fifteen, about ten and a half stone, and I was a tomboy and never had anything about me, very plain.

Robby Baron was true to his word and gave me a try. He threw me about a bit in the ring and said, 'If you're really interested, come back in a fortnight' – thought he'd got rid of me. Two weeks later I got in again with another wrestler – Tony Francis. He picked me up, threw me on the floor and broke my ankle.

I went to stay with an aunt in Blackpool, and went down every day to learn with professionals. It was a concrete floor in a garage with posts. They threw me around, and I was black and blue. I trained with a lot of fellas, but the main ones were Mighty John

Quinn and Adrian Street. His wife was another wrestler, another Indian, but she was a *real* Indian.

I learnt all the basics, how to fall, how to protect myself, all the holds. Half of the holds I learnt don't even exist now. But the main thing is learning how to fall without breaking your back. Most of the training you learn is never enough compared to what you learn in your head – how to manipulate the crowd, and manipulate who you're on with. Now I think I'm the best not because of my holds, but because I know how to work the crowd. The crowd don't want wrestling, just pure wrestling. I don't think I could wrestle cleanly if I tried. I just like winding them up, and the more I do it the better I feel.

If people have never seen women's wrestling they think, Oh boobs out, bum out. But it's not like that at all. We don't really wrestle the same as men. We're more catty, but then women are generally more catty than men. Cattier.

My partner Frank is disabled. He used to be perfectly able-bodied, building trucks and wagons – welding. His kidneys failed, and they gave him a course of steroids. The steroids wrecked his body so much. We've been together three and a half years. I might get married one day. I'd like to get married in the ring, but he wouldn't do it because he's very shy. A lot of people think that if you're a girl wrestler you're a lesbian. There's so much crap that's written about women in sport.

Miss Linda: Basically I got work because I was reliable, and a lot of the other girls weren't. The other girls didn't really like my image, Blackfoot Sue. I began at a time when most of the others were just in old leotards, no fancy costumes. To your face they were all right, but behind your back they were catty – a lot of jealousy. Not just me – all the girls were suspicious of each other.

I didn't mind being hated in the ring. Me and Adrian are still the mixed-tag champions, and they hated us. They began hating us when I was his valet. They used to go mad when, if there weren't stairs, I let him step on my back to get in the ring.

Klondyke Kate: It used to be more violent than it is now. Not the wrestling, the crowd participation. Years ago it was very bad. I was stabbed on my hand with a knife. That was in a music hall in Aberdeen. The crowd was so incensed by what was going on, which wasn't much, but they just used to go off like a bottle of pop. A fellow came at me with either a Stanley knife or a vegetable knife. But I thought that I had got him like that – it was my fault, I've got a lot of gob – so I couldn't do too much about it. I think they took him away and he was prosecuted by the police.

The wrestlers could be almost as bad. Worse. At the beginning I had so many diabolical things done to me. I've been chucked in a chip shop, stripped off. Locked in rooms. I've had my suitcase nailed to the floor and almost broke my neck as I tried to lift it. That was Frank Casey, the British Bushwhacker.

I didn't meet Mitzi for twelve months. They all lived in the Manchester area – a hard place, Manchester. I felt sick fighting them, terrified of making a fool of myself. I *was* sick too. I thought,

Adrian Street and Miss Linda: 'I let him step on my back to get in the ring'

What am I doing here – I could go and work in a factory. But if I hadn't been a wrestler I don't think I would have ever come out of Stoke-on-Trent. My mum did eight to five, and when she came home she was shattered. I worked in her factory, Johnson Brothers, on the pottery line where my mum actually worked, and I couldn't take it.

I can't explain to you how much I loved wrestling in the early days. It certainly wasn't the money. It was the lifestyle, travelling everywhere, going abroad. I went on my own to Nigeria when I was sixteen to wrestle an American girl. I went to Japan for six weeks in '82, when I was nineteen and a bit wiser, though not as wise as I am today. I did thirty-six venues in forty days. I came back with loads of money. I could have bought a house with everything I earnt. But I gave it all away to my relatives or friends, or I spent it.

Now I'm sick to the teeth of travelling, I hate it.

When I'm in the ring I get a buzz – everybody will say this. The attention is on you, it's fantastic. Out of the wrestling I'm a completely different person. Because of my weight I'm embarrassed to go swimming with my children, and yet I stand up and wrestle in front of hundreds, and I'm not one bit ashamed when I've got my wrestling costume on. I don't care what they think I look like, because I feel brilliant. Nothing can harm me.

When I'm myself, when I'm walking around, I think people are staring at me, and I don't like it. And I know people stare, and always do at large people. My armour is to bite back and be nasty, before they hurt me.

Like a lot of wrestlers I'm very temperamental. I can be deliriously happy one minute, and totally unhappy the next. I can be like that at home. I'm very hard to live with, either happy or totally depressed. A lot of wrestlers are like that. One time you can talk to Haystacks and he'll be as nice as pie and the next he'll bite your head off, it doesn't matter who you are.

When I started people called me Big Bertha and I hated it. They always call large people that, don't they? But then I got used to it, and I had a T-shirt printed with Big Bertha on it. You do silly things like that when you start, having your name on things. Tony Francis, the person who broke my ankle, said, 'You're not going to keep that name.' I said, 'I am. It's my name. It's what I'm going to be.'

I said that Big Bertha was the name that my bosses said I had to be. I got into this raging row, and in the end he had me crying about it. A few weeks later Bobby Barron came up with this Klondyke Kate. I'd heard the name but I wasn't sure where, and later I found out that Klondyke Kate was a saloon owner in Canada. It just had a ring about it, I thought people would remember it. I started lying about it, saying my dad was from the Klondyke. My dad was never from the Klondyke – he was from Stoke-on-Trent.

The make-up is just something not to make me look too washed out under the lights. The more I put on, the harder I look. I began just in plain leotard costumes, but once, after watching the Americans, I went out in some chains and bits of leather hanging off, and the reaction was great, and I thought, That's it. Since then all the girls got special costumes.

No one would remember me if I used my real name – Jane Porter. I get quite offended at wrestling shows when people come up and call me by my real name. When I'm wrestling I'm Kate. Jane Porter is Jane Porter with her children and family. But people come up after a show and say, 'Hello Jane, how's the baby?' What's it to them? I don't care about their children.

When I started we couldn't wrestle in London at all. We finally got in eight years ago – practically my first job back after having my son. It was Mitzi's farewell.

Mitzi Mueller: I worked in London at the clubs, for private shows, but never ever in a hall, because the halls couldn't get the licence. They just didn't want us because we were women. They were stopping me doing my job.

The Times Law Report, 21 November 1979: A woman professional wrestler who was refused employment by a promotions company because of a provision in a Greater London Council Licence prohibiting women's wrestling was not unlawfully discriminated against because of her sex.

Mr Justice Slynn said that the applicant, Mrs Marjorie Farrar,

39, of Pudsey, near Leeds, who wrestles as Sue Brittain, had asked Verdun Leslie Promotions for an engagement. They refused, saying that the wrestling licence issued by the GLC governing wrestling at Manor Place Baths, Southwark, had a condition prohibiting women from taking part.

Mrs Farrar's husband, Ronald, had told the tribunal that wrestling was his wife's source of income, and this was being affected by the GLC's refusal to allow her to compete in public halls.

Ken Livingstone: It was banned on the grounds that it was degrading to women. You're asking me to remember how I felt about something that happened more than fifteen years ago? I supported it. I would ban boxing too. Women's wrestling always had a sexual innuendo and content to it.

Mitzi Mueller: There were all sorts of shows going on in London, sex shows and everything, and my wrestling was not a sex show. So I made a noise about it. I made a record, 'Let The Girls In (To London Town)'. It sold very well, it's quite good actually. The backing group was Suzi Quatro's band. The words were very good, and it got onto every local radio station. 'Let the girls into London town / We want to fight but they're putting us down / . . .' I can't remember the rest.

By this time I'd been wrestling for twenty-five years. One day we arrived at a hall to hear we'd got the go ahead and the ban had been lifted. I said to Brian, 'That's it, then, I want the final big one – the Royal Albert Hall.' That had been my ambition all the time I'd been wrestling. It had always been the big venue, where Prince Philip and the Duke of Kent had come.

There were people there I hadn't seen for years, people with flowers and people with presents. I remember being terribly nervous, shaking. I won the contest. It was a tag: Rusty Blair was my partner, against Klondyke Kate and Nicky Monroe. When we won, I looked round and everyone was cheering and crying, I was crying, the referee was crying. And then the bells went, the timekeeper rang ten bells and that was heartbreaking. Out of respect.

There was a young girl just started in the business, I forget her name, and I presented her with my jacket.

Peter Blake: Because of the ban I only saw the women when I lived down in Somerset. In a club I saw a woman wrestle a man, probably husband and wife. It wasn't a sex show, but it was veering towards it.

I saw that last fight at the Albert Hall, Mitzi Mueller's farewell. She passed on her cape to her daughter, I think – quite emotional. It was a good night, but it was only half full which was a bit sad. You felt the promoters were giving it the very best they could. It was Kendo, John Quinn, Klondyke Kate and all good fights. But the punters just didn't come, so I think the promoters realized it was over. If they wouldn't come to that at the Albert Hall, it was clear it was eventually going to die.

Brian Dixon: The Albert Hall was not licensed by the GLC – it had its own licence. The biggest mistake was that we put it on the Friday night, and people are leaving town. I think we got about a thousand – nothing in the Albert Hall. It ran overtime and I had to pay another £300 for half an hour.

I don't encourage her to talk about her days because she does miss the job very much. She retired because of injury. Her back was absolutely knackered. At the end she was in hospital more times

Mitzi Mueller outside the Royal Albert Hall:
'I was crying, the referee was crying'

than she was out. Two bones in her back were just rubbing away at each other, and it got so bad that in the end I said to her, 'Look, there's not enough money in this job for you to go through the pain you've got.'

Mitzi Mueller: I go to the local shows and the atmosphere has gone. A lot of wrestlers aren't dedicated, they don't give as we did. Some are good, but I look at a lot of them and I think, How embarrassing. They don't take as much pride in themselves. They think they can just turn up.

I'm glad I got out before I ended at the bottom again. I'm still recognized in supermarkets. A woman came up to me with tears in her eyes and said, 'Oh my gosh, I can't believe it, after all these years . . .' Recently we went to a charity do in Liverpool and Lily Savage was sat on the next table. I could see him looking, and then when someone called me Mitzi he said, 'I *thought* it was you – I used to go see you at the Stadium and I used to love you.'

Klondyke Kate: When Mitzi finished we did the 40 *Minutes* television programme, me and Nicky Monroe, an eliminator for Mitzi's belt. This was at the end of the eighties. The girl who did the film, Alison Parisio, won a bursary to do it, and originally when she came to me I said no, because everyone who does anything about wrestling takes the piss, and I don't like it. It's not fair – we work very hard.

But then I let her come round with us for three months. At the end she said I could come to the editing room in London, and she said if there was anything on the tape I didn't like she would cut it out. The only thing I didn't like was this one scene. My little boy bit a little girl off-camera, and I then bit my little boy. That's how I've always worked. Adam bit one of my friend's children, so I bit Adam to let him know it hurts. But because he bit her off-camera, and I bit him on-camera, it wasn't right. It made me look like a child biter. He was crying, and I didn't like that. So they cut that out.

When I was younger the thought of finishing wrestling was akin to dying. Knowing that one day what you love is going to end is so shattering. But when you get older it doesn't mean as much. If you would have said to me ten years ago that I would have had children, I would have said no chance – it would interfere. I don't go away like I used to. I've only been away a day and I miss my kids desperately. Not so much the father, but my kids.

I really don't want to wrestle so much any more. I've had enough. I've put so much weight on in the last seven years. In a way it's done me a lot of good. It's kept my face in this business.

Initially the male wrestlers didn't accept women. But now I'm very much one of the lads. I've never really liked female company, only male company. Years ago I used to drink, not any more, but I still like to sit with the lads and play pool. They've really accepted me over the years, and I love that. That's meant more to me than anything, being respected by wrestlers.

Even Les Kellett would talk to me like the others, which wasn't exactly nice. He was very very funny in the ring. He was horrible outside the ring . . . I can't put into words how horrible he was. Everyone was frightened of him. He had these hands . . . We were in Plymouth, and I couldn't take my eyes off these hands – like a shovel. All I could think was that I'd hate him to slap me with those hands. He'd just grunt at you. I went into a fish and chip shop with him once and he wanted this fish, and because it didn't turn out the way he wanted he just chucked it at the man, straight in the face. He spoke his mind. I liked all the old timers.

I've never said I was retiring before. I told a wrestler last night and he said, 'I don't believe you,' but I mean it. When I finish I've got to throw my boots away. I've only got one pair of boots, but twenty costumes, many of which I can't get into. I just want to be with my family now, and I don't want to work any more.

Simon Garfield, Letter 29 November 1995:

Dear Les,

It is now over two months since I first wrote, and still no sign of life. Pat Roach told me earlier this week that someone had spotted you at a local market, and that you looked fit and well. If only I could confirm this with my own eyes.

I understand that a man with your history might be reluctant to talk to a stranger for nothing. With this in mind, I would like to offer you a fee for your time. How does £100 cash sound?

I only need a short period of any day you name. Such time would be treasured, and of value not only to me but to thousands throughout the country, all of whom I imagine to be eager to hear from you again. Though this may be hard for you to appreciate, your ring exploits still stir the fondest memories, and it would be a great shame if these were allowed to slip from view, washed over by so much that passes for popular entertainment these days.

In case you've mislaid my original requests, I'm the bloke who's writing about wrestling.

With very best wishes.

Joe D'Orazio: I got a lovely letter from Les saying how sorry he was not to be able to come to the reunion. He said that since his wife left him, he had to look after his animals. He keeps chickens. Les was the hardest of them all, I'd say. He could kill people just by looking at them. People were terrified of Les, and look what a kind letter he wrote me. He wrote that he was a little worried about how the other wrestlers would react to him after all these years. It was great to hear from him.

11

'I'm going to have to talk eventually,' said Kendo Nagasaki

Kendo Nagasaki and Peter Blake:
'You're not supposed to touch the mask'

Max Crabtree: I read in the *Evening Standard* that there was an exhibition at the Tate Gallery of an artist, and it said that amongst some of his work were some unusual paintings of a masked wrestler. I thought, 'Who the bloody hell is this?'

So I nipped over to the Tate, and lo and behold, it was the Zebra Kid. A terrific masked man, he was an American, George Borless, and he wrestled all over the world and eventually ended up in this country. He was the most grotesque masked man you could imagine. He was about five foot nine and weighed about twenty-eight stone. He had this enormous girth, and terrific balance.

Tate Gallery Catalogue 1983, *Masked Zebra Kid*, 1965: this is probably the only real-life wrestler in the series. The signature in the centre is an autograph signed by the wrestler for the artist. The head has been deliberately darkened.

Max Crabtree: The artist was a bit of an oddball, but was obviously a very good wrestling fan. Obviously he had this thing about masked men. Some very bizarre paintings.

Peter Blake: I told my fellow students about the wrestling, but I would have hesitated to tell the teachers. They would have looked down on it. That's always been odd about my work – I lived this double cultural life. During the day I was being taught about Rembrandt, high culture, and one evening a week I'd be going to the wrestling and one evening I'd be going to the modern jazz club and hearing bebop. Then when I got to the Royal College, that's what Pop Art was: suddenly I thought my life was quite interesting – I'll paint about that.

When I started my wrestlers I'd already been recognized as a pop artist. This was in the mid- to late fifties. They were nice pictures, almost always well received. They were usually fictitious wrestlers. I would use some real names but change the image, or use the images of real wrestlers and change their names, like with Doktor K Tortur. The only real one I painted was the Zebra Kid, and that only because I got his autograph.

I went to Hammersmith, a match at the cinema there, now gone, and I happened to be walking past the stage door when he came out. The mask was still on, an enormous man, with a rather old-fashioned gabardine coat, like a schoolboy's coat, but gigantic. A little boy went up and said, 'Will you sign this?' and he went 'No!' and pushed him away, being a real villain. I thought, Well, shall I ask him?, and so I offered him something to sign, and in an American accent he said, 'Yeah, I know you.' He meant from the ringside. He wouldn't have known I was a painter. But he signed this paper, and I built the picture around that.

Something like the Da Vinci Brothers painting would obviously have been an art joke as well – an Italian tag team. I liked to confuse the imagery. Like I did Franck and Jesse, the James Brothers, but they looked like Germans. I liked all that mythology and all those mistakes. I had one called Pretty Boy Michael Angelo, who was modelled on a photograph of a skinhead. At the show I used to love the Wild Man of Borneo for the incongruity of it – he had all this hair and all this grunting rage, but then underneath you could see these little maroon trunks with the logo of a diver on.

Ian Dury: On a Wednesday night in early September 1961, Peter Blake walked into the third-year painting room at Walthamstow School of Art. Blue tab-collar shirt, silk paisley tie, herringbone jacket and gold beard. He looked like the front man of the modern art quartet. I was painting a humdrum scene in a slipshod manner and looking forward to going down the Bell.

'Do you like rock 'n' roll?' he asked.

'Yes.'

'Boxing and wrestling?'

'Yes, and tits and bums, gangsters, teddy boys, Jayne Mansfield and Marlon Brando.'

'Then why don't you paint pictures of what you like?'

Peter Blake: I didn't really mix with the wrestlers socially. Johnny Yearsley was a life model at Gravesend, so I met him. Sometimes you'd see them drinking in the local pub afterwards. But often I preferred to believe the myth.

As a painter I'm always intrigued by the edges of society, the fringes of entertainment. This is based on the principle that there is no such thing as perfection, no perfect thing or perfect body. Thus something that's imperfect is valid just because it's imperfect. I'm not fetishistic about it – I'm not interested in amputees. That's why I was so intrigued by wrestling, and dwarf wrestlers are always interesting. They play it like midget circus clowns, more or less as comedy, although they're incredibly skilled. The troupe I saw included Sky Lo Lo who had the shaven head, there was Fuzzy Cupid who had a mad halo of white hair, quite elderly, there was Little Beaver the Red Indian, and there was a Russian, Ivan something, who came in in a Cossack outfit. It was extreme theatre. They would run under the ref's legs, and at first they would only wrestle each other, but then later a midget tag team would take on a normal-sized wrestler.

And I was always fascinated by masked wrestlers, though there were very few good ones in England. Nagasaki, Count Bartelli, the White Ranger and Dr Death. Then a couple on the edges like the Red Scorpion. One rumour was that a very prominent member of the Royal Family was a masked professional wrestler. Another apparently was a famous surgeon. Another was so horrifically disfigured that you would faint if you saw his face. But even then you knew that this man would change in the dressing room and pull off his mask and go home in a suit on the bus.

Brian Glover: Once I went to the tax office and an inspector said to me, 'Mr Glover, you've been very honest with us. Just one more thing,' and he paused, and I thought, Oh no – it's going to be something awful.

Then he said, 'Can you tell us who Dr Death is?'

Mal Sanders: Dr Death was Paul Lincoln. Most of the time. One night in Saffron Walden Paul didn't show up so they asked John Elijah to do it. John is a huge man, his lats are so big that his arms stick out, walks like he's carrying two rolls of lino. So they get a mask for him, and they announce him as Dr Death, and as he walks out to this packed audience someone in the crowd shouts, 'Hello John!', and John goes, ''Allo love, how are you?'

Peter Blake: In the sixties they used to put wrestling on at the Metropolitan Theatre in the Edgware Road. The ring was on the stage, and they wrestled out into the hall. There was a series of grudge matches between Dr Death and the White Angel, very much black and white. On this particular night Dr Death fell to the ground and said, 'I've been shot!' There was consternation, but one quickly realized he hadn't been shot very much – he wasn't dead or anything. The stewards came running towards where I was sitting, and there was a youth next to me who ran off, and the person sitting on the other side of me said, 'He had an airgun!' The attendants rushed up and thought I'd done it, because it came from that exact spot. They said, 'Come on, we know it was you, come with us.' I said, 'I didn't, I didn't, it was that little boy who'd run off.'

It was very dramatic. For a moment it was like an assassination. But it soon turned to farce. They quickly realized it wasn't me. But the shooting wasn't rehearsed or part of the show – I think it was just a White Angel fan who had a grudge against Dr Death.

Dr Death: 'Dr Death was Paul Lincoln. Most of the time'

Lloyd Ryan: Paul Lincoln was a fair-haired Australian with a very clever eye for business and showmanship. He would put on his own bills, tear the tickets, sell the drinks, then go round the back, put the mask on and come back out as Dr Death. Top of the bill. But we also know what else Paul Lincoln did – Paul owned the Two I's coffee bar and had the opportunity of managing Cliff Richard and Tommy Steele, and didn't take it.

When I first saw Kendo Nagasaki I thought, What a great idea. That red mask with the white stripes – no one knew who he was. People followed him, but goodness knows why. It was like following the faceless man: it wasn't as if it was Mick McManus or Steve Logan under there. He had always been consistent. Most masked wrestlers had just been in for a year or two and then unmasked. Everyone knew who they were – the Outlaw, Dr Death, the Zebra Kid. But with Kendo no one knew. There was no background to the man.

Peter Blake: I wanted to believe that Kendo was really Japanese. Even when I worked with him I still didn't want to know too much. So after we talked on the phone I thought that I'm not going to tell you very much about Kendo. That would veer towards the exposé, and I'm not interested in that.

The *Sunday Times Magazine* did an article called Linking the Chain of Envy, where they asked a doctor what he would have been if he hadn't been a doctor. He said he would have liked to have been an artist. Then they contacted me and asked me what I would have been if not a painter. The point was to go on until you'd get to someone who wanted to be a doctor, and the chain would be complete.

When they contacted me I thought I would have liked to have been a joiner of some kind or a woodworker. But then I thought that what I would really like to have been was a wrestler. Specifically, I said, I would love to experience being Kendo Nagasaki. I always thought he was totally separate from the rest. There was a kind of genuineness about him. In the article I mentioned that I wondered how he made his eyes so red. Then Kendo wanted to be Richard Branson, who wanted to be a journalist.

Some years afterwards this television producer from Belfast contacted me. He said he was a wrestling fan, that I was his favourite painter, that Kendo was his favourite wrestler and that his fantasy was to wrestle him. He's a madman, Paul Yates – his fantasy was actually to wrestle Kendo. They were both into martial arts and the same sort of Eastern mythology.

That's how the *Arena* programme came about. Paul tried to set up a meeting, and initially they wouldn't. You've talked to Lloyd Ryan, so you know how difficult he can be. Finally they agreed, and we went to a bungalow Kendo had in south London.

Lloyd let us in, and I thought Lloyd was Kendo, without his mask on. We talked to Lloyd for half an hour, and then he said, 'Mr Nagasaki will see you now.' After a while he came in in day clothes, a rather nice cashmere sweater, with black shoes and gold chains, but with the mask on. It was the black mask. He actually goes through a transition. He begins with the black mask, and gradually becomes Kendo Nagasaki, and then he puts on the red mask.

He sat there for about an hour and wouldn't talk. We carried on talking to Lloyd, and finally Kendo said, 'I'm going to have to talk eventually, aren't I?' He had a deep voice, ever so slightly gruff. 'If we make this film I'm going to have to communicate with you. I've never done an interview in my life, and I won't do one now, but I'll talk to you in the making of the film.' So from then on, without the mask he would talk to us, with the black mask he would talk to us, but only once with the red mask. That was when he had to.

Kendo Nagasaki: I don't do anything to make my eyes appear red. It's just a look. Richard Branson is the person I'd like to be. His is

Nagasaki unmasked by Gorgeous George: 'It was a sensation'

a remarkable career. He started from a phone box and built an empire. He lives his life on the edge, up front, taking risks. He's not one of these faceless magnates who hides behind the frosted windows of a limousine. You feel that he's accessible, that he's a person of the people.

Lloyd Ryan: I've lost weight since that film was made. Two stone. I wished I had lost a bit of weight then, and wasn't so much of the fat old tortoise.

With Kendo it's going back years. I began just as a fan, and then I brought out a record called 'Kendo's Theme', a drumming instrumental. That came out about 1975, and got in the top hundred. Massive airplay – about five hundred spins on local radio, because they used to play it in the background as a voice-over. We recorded it as 'Lloyd Ryan's Express', like Von Ryan's Express. Up to that point I had been doing well as a drummer – working with P. J. Proby, Gene Vincent, Edmundo Ross, Matt Monroe – but my name was unknown. After 'Kendo's Theme' I made three tuition LPs and I got a tutor book out. So good for me, and marvellous for Kendo. They played it as an entrance theme when he went into the ring. The wrestling fans bought it. Looking back, it wasn't such a great record, it was okay. Me and Kendo went all over together doing local radio shows. He never spoke at all. He then had a manager called George Gillette, Gorgeous George, and he spoke for him.

Then many years later, when George retired and then died, Kendo also retired for a bit, and came into my business, the music business. He managed several bands – I think he helped manage the Cuddly Toys. No one in the business really knew about his wrestling. This was in the late seventies, early eighties.

Then in about 1988 I got a phone-call, and Kendo asked me whether I would represent him in the ring. I said I'd love to do it, but I didn't know whether I could or not, because George had a very camp image. I was more aggressive. I was disliked, really hated. George they just laughed at.

Max Crabtree: I remember advising Kendo about getting a manager. When he started out, he already had the mask but he was getting nowhere. We were coming back in the Transit van with the rest of the wrestlers on the bill from Edinburgh, this must have been the early seventies, and he was really down because he was making no impact with all the Japanese stuff, and he didn't know where to turn. I suggested having a manager, someone who would accompany him in the ring – a well-worn trick in America. So I introduced him to George Gillette – Gorgeous George – the manager of the Theatre Royal in Halifax, near my farm. Kendo thought he was marvellous, the perfect extrovert.

I was Kendo's rabbi. George was just the right man, because with a masked man of course he was a faceless person. A manager has to put the verbals to it. And of course with George being a homosexual and needing no prompting to show it . . . Our audience was mostly working class, and they hated homosexuality.

If there's one thing that Kendo was, he was very professional. Whether he was homosexual he's never shown. In all the years I knew him he's very much a man's man in every way. Obviously George was inclined to be that way, and the wrestlers would throw scorn on him. In Kendo's case, well I heard all these things.

Robbie Brookside: Once Kendo was in the ring at Imperial College, and the students began chanting, 'Kendo takes it up the arse, doo-dah, doo-dah!' That really got him mad.

Max Crabtree: He lived in a most beautiful house with about an acre of garden in Wolverhampton. Worth about £300,000, beautifully furnished. He'd been very lucky. He had an adopted aunt, or she had adopted him, who had a few properties up and down the country, in Blackpool and the Midlands. When she died, Kendo had got the lot, which had given him a lot of independence. It's one of those fairytale stories – we'd all like to have an auntie like that.

Kendo was one of those men who knew what was what and where he was going. A very forthright man. He said what he thought. A lot of the wrestlers behind the scenes were a little bit wary of him. I wouldn't say he was the favourite of the team.

Whenever it was humanly possible I put him in a dressing room on his own. There was such heat on him. I sat talking to him one day, and he had a phobia about anyone coming in the dressing room. From the moment he arrived at the hall he'd have the mask on. But when he got in the dressing room, because he often went on third, and might be there for a couple of hours, he'd lift the mask half-way up. He had this fear if he couldn't lock the door, and in a lot of civic halls the fire regulations dictated that you couldn't. I remember on one occasion the hall manager was looking for me, and I'm sat with Kendo. So the manager comes into the dressing room – it was his building after all, so he didn't think there was anything wrong. But as he came through the door, Kendo jumped up and trapped the manager's head in the door.

Keeping his identity intact was an obsession. You'd never once catch Kendo in the bar. Half of these wrestlers were supposed to have kicked the shit out of each other and then they'd lounge in the bar together. Never Kendo.

He told me at the time when he was first approached to do that programme and said, 'I'm interested in doing it, but anything that would be derogatory to wrestling I won't do.' So he had meetings with the company who were going to make it, and told them, 'Unless you do it my way, and keep the mystique of it, then I'm not interested.' And it came out that way.

Peter Blake: The film was going to have other wrestlers in it, but it changed, and became far more mystical. I had met Brian Glover before at the Chelsea Arts Club, where we talked wrestling. He's interested in talking about it, but he'll never expose it. He told me about his shoot, that's what they call a genuine fight. For the film we met at Langan's to talk about wrestlers, and there was quite a lot of alcohol consumed. The other thing was he had two lunches. He ordered an enormous plate of sausage and mash, which he ate during filming. But then we had to reshoot, and he had to eat it again.

Brian Glover: We were there just to talk about wrestling in general, but it ran late into the afternoon and Peter kept on eating, and we both kept on drinking and in the end Peter could hardly speak. All they had on the tape was me talking about my mother's washing line and Peter going 'Ken . . . do . . . Naaagaaas . . .'

Peter Blake: I left the wrestling with Kendo one night. Driving to

Brian Glover
with Peter Blake:
'In the end, Peter
could hardly speak'

a match he puts on the mask about a mile from the venue, and driving away he takes it off also about a mile away, in case he's being followed. The first time I saw him without a mask we left not with Lloyd driving, but his assistant Laurence. I could see the back of his head, but not his face.

For the film Kendo got me dressed in his clothes, and I walked out from the dressing room one afternoon before a match at Stoke, with the mask on, and the metal mask and the cloak and the sword, incredibly cumbersome, and I did the strut, and stood under the lights, and for one second or two I actually was Kendo Nagasaki. They didn't use it in the film.

I don't want to destroy the Kendo myth with anything that's gossipy, but I do know he was a judoka of world championship class, and went to Japan and certainly has one finger cut off. In Japan it's the sign of a cult, the equivalent of the mafia. Terence Donovan the photographer, who's also a six-Dan judoka, can remember seeing a judo fight in Japan in which a young English wrestler beat the then champion of the world, a Finn. Terence deduced that it must have been Kendo.

Max Crabtree: The Mafia? Kendo used to be an apprentice at Jennings, the horse-box makers in Crewe. That's where he got the finger severed off.

Lloyd Ryan: With Kendo people were convinced that there were several Kendos. But I can put this on record now and say there was actually only one – for the whole period of time. The public are wildly wrong. They all have offbeat ideas – all these little hypotheses, even last year when I did the *Danny Baker Show* and Kendo played the drums, and they were saying it wasn't the real Kendo, but it *was* the real Kendo. Only ever one Kendo – that's what makes it fairly unique. People would come up to me and say, 'I think you're the real Kendo.' When I was fatter I was more his size. They'd say, 'We never saw you and Kendo together at the same time,' but that's rubbish, we were together all the time. That's the wrestling public for you, not too many Einsteins.

There was an article twenty years ago about masked wrestlers which said that everyone had been unmasked – Count Bartelli, the Zebra Kid, the Red Scorpion – but not Kendo. The article said that it would be sad if he ever did get unmasked and finished, and we knew who he was and what he had for breakfast and what he had for dinner. It's like Hitler: did Hitler really die in 1945, did he really poison and shoot himself? – there's always this little bit of doubt. That's what's nice about Kendo, one of the few wrestlers who disappeared into the mists of time. He could be someone upstairs watching the telly for all you know. It's nice that there's a little bit of mystery in life, like the Loch Ness monster.

On the *Danny Baker Show*, Baker expected him to roll up in the afternoon and say, 'Hello mate!', but none of that. The first he saw

Lloyd Ryan with Nagasaki: 'If Kendo's going to play a musical instrument, it can't be the violin'

of him was when we walked down the steps on the show. Kendo just sat there, and Baker said during the programme that he was the only chat show host to have a guest who didn't talk. Funniest moment of the evening, apart from the drumming.

Kendo plays a couple of beats and things. If Kendo's going to play a musical instrument, it can't be the violin. Kendo's as good on the drums as I am a wrestler, and I've still got marks from that.

I did a couple of tag matches with Kendo, but I just virtually stood and watched while everyone else just fought around me. The first time was along the pier at Worthing, against Pete Roberts and Robbie Brookside. Kendo really carried me. I just stood on the apron and punched someone now and again. With the wrestling I had no idea what I was doing.

It's a lot tougher than people realize. When they come off the ropes and they bodycheck each other, that ring moves. When they hit you . . . everyone thinks they don't touch each other but believe me they do. I can promise you that when they get in that ring they do hit each other. It would look ridiculous otherwise. If they just went 'ping' people wouldn't stand for it.

I fought just out of box-office demand. The promoter just thought it was very gimmicky to have the manager in there, getting his come-uppance. Didn't matter that I couldn't wrestle – the public demanded to see me getting my head kicked in. The promoter agreed: give the public what they want.

At the peak of it we almost had riots. One of our great opponents was Rollerball Rocco. We've had bloodbaths with Rollerball Rocco and the crowds at the end were like a Wembley Cup Final. But in those days you could have put Kendo on against a broomstick and they would have watched.

Max Crabtree: Lloyd Ryan wasn't like George. Kendo and George were like Abbott and Costello.

So it's winter, and they have a leak in the bathroom. George, who actually lived with Kendo at this time, looked in the Yellow Pages for a plumber. He finds one, and the guy comes round and George opens the door. I think this is late seventies.

Now the plumber turns out to be a wrestling nut. Much to the plumber's amazement, he turns up at this house, and there in front of him is his great hero, George Gillette. The plumber doesn't say anything. So he goes in, and George says, 'Peter, the plumber is here.' The guy reading the newspaper on the couch is Kendo Nagasaki without a mask.

Now the plumber puts two and two together. There were no women in the house. The plumber realizes he's seen the real McCoy, and he's got the name of the resident of the house – Peter Thornley – because they'd given that to pay for the bill.

Now, one night soon after we're in the Civic Hall, Wolverhampton. Peter's on the bill, and in the dressing room. One of the wrestlers comes lounging in, I think it's Pat Roach, and says, 'Max, have you seen these leaflets? There's two fellows at the door giving out these bloody leaflets.'

I say, 'Let's have a look,' and it says on it, 'The wrestler Kendo Nagasaki is Peter Thornley and he lives at this address . . .'

I thought, 'Them bastards! Where the hell are they?' So I shoot to the front door, and the two guys must have known I had something to do with it, because they throw the leaflets up in the air and go racing down the road.

For the next few weeks, wherever we have a show within a forty-mile radius of Wolverhampton these people . . . they are getting really cunning now with these leaflets, and are giving them to other people to give out. But it didn't make any difference. Because had Peter Thornley been Les Kellett before he put the mask on, then it would have meant something. But Peter Thornley didn't mean anything to nobody.

But this guy and his friends became a bloody nuisance. On one occasion I grabbed him and said, 'Look, don't be a silly fellow, it's stupid what you're doing – you're just bloody annoying everybody.' He was a wrestling nut, and because Kendo was a villain, it was like his way of getting his own back.

Kendo would have murdered the bastard. Killed him. But he couldn't do, because he had all this heat on him, the star of the show, and he can't go running down the high street with his Samurai sword. This was in the period when Kendo was having his best run.

It didn't end there. This fellow decided he would invest all of his money not just in printing leaflets. He knew that we advertised in the local paper, the *Express and Star*. So when the advertisement for a Kendo Nagasaki bout appeared in the paper, underneath it would be a smaller advert that this plumber had paid for: 'Please note that the above wrestler, Kendo Nagasaki, is Peter Thornley and lives at this address . . .'

So enough was enough. The plumber ended up in the local magistrates court. We'd got his address, and put an injunction on him to stop him from doing it again. The plumber doesn't turn up at the court. He sends a letter in, and says he's very sorry, it won't happen again.

Peter Blake: For a while Kendo did wrestle simply without a mask. He told me he never actually lost. He was disqualified, and he didn't always win, but he never actually lost. When he fought Count Bartelli, Bartelli had to unmask because he was the loser. But when Kendo did it the first time he just chose to do so. And because you had no idea who it was, it was weirder.

Max Crabtree: In the end, he decided he just wanted to unmask by himself. Most masked wrestlers, as they get older, they want the public to know who they are. It's like the little man inside . . . they want everybody to know.

Count Bartelli had been a marvellous masked man, mostly around the north of England, before television. He wanted to unmask, but I said to him – his name was Jeff – I said, 'Jeff, you're a silly fellow, you don't have to reveal yourself.' But he got involved in a big match at the Victoria Hall with Kendo – the master and the pupil. A titanic struggle. He wanted to unmask at the end. If you lose you can still keep the mask on – you can. But it was an inner thing – he wanted the world to know that behind that mask was this face.

Kendo did take his mask off too, towards the end. To me that was wrong. Peter and I had slight differences. He felt I was taking him too deeply into it. They were getting worried: with George there was so much heat on him that he couldn't come out of the dressing room – the fans would have burnt George on a stake. If you couldn't come out of the dressing room it would spoil the routine.

So he toyed with the idea of unmasking, but I said, 'Peter . . .' He didn't have a very unusual face. He was just a nice-looking sort of guy, but nothing significant. But he was so determined to unmask that we decided to do it properly, at the Wolverhampton Civic Hall where he was hottest.

Because he lived in this twilight world, he had always had hangers-on around him, these strange oddballs, culty types that he called his acolytes.

Brian Crabtree: They were two sandwiches short of a picnic.

Max Crabtree: These guys were quite dangerous, because most people in the hall couldn't stand Kendo, and then we had this crazy lot supporting him, and opposing the crowd, so we had to go in really strong to keep them apart. Half a dozen of these guys were around him for the unmasking, but he let George take off the actual mask very slowly. Kendo was on his knees, and as he looked up, there on his head was this occult tattoo, which with his red eyes made him look absolutely powerful. It was a sensation.

Peter Blake: He had this completely shaven head, with a tattooed star on the top, and a pony-tail that really was like a horse's tail because it grew out of a small circle of hair. And this face, which was oriental, or Mongolian.

Kent Walton: That tattoo . . . no wonder he wore a mask.

Max Crabtree: Eventually he left me, and went to Brian. He totally domineered Brian. Brian was frightened of him. I'm not running Brian Dixon down. I've no need to. The days are over. But with Brian, Kendo could do what the hell he wanted.

What I was worried about with Peter, is that sometimes in his matches if he went in with a young fellow, he'd brutalize him. He had that in him . . . if they weren't just good enough he would literally annihilate them. This would make the audience very ugly, and I didn't like that.

With the mask he realized he had made a mistake afterwards. He told me it wasn't right. I told him at the time, 'You're making a mistake, kid – all that good work that you've put in, you'll lose it all.' And he did do. It took the shine off him.

Peter Blake: You did see a bit of his face towards the end of the *Arena* programme, in the fight with Haystacks.

Lloyd Ryan: The heavyweight championship match against Giant Haystacks at Fairfield Halls – we thought we were going to win that. But we lost it. The BBC were very upset about that. But what can you do with Haystacks? He was the giant.

One thing that wasn't on the film: the Wrestling Board of Control, i.e. Brian Dixon and his cronies, decided they wanted Pat Roach as the referee. But the last thing we wanted was Pat Roach as the referee, because he was one of our biggest rivals. I spent about half an hour saying that there will be no championship match if you don't get rid of this bloke. So we got rid of Pat Roach, and got in Steve Grey, who was neither here nor there, a little light-weight. But Pat Roach – no way, too biased. That was the power of Kendo – we overruled Brian Dixon. Normally the promoter's word is final. Normally if you don't do as you're told for Brian or Max Crabtree you're out.

Peter Blake: I do admire Haystacks, but I don't think you can be both a Haystacks fan and a Nagasaki fan. I think he's much better than he used to be. There was a time when if the fight went on for more than twelve seconds, Haystacks simply couldn't go on. But when he fought Kendo he genuinely got as fit as he could. That fight was as close as you got to a shoot. The only way Kendo could beat him was if he could tire Haystacks out. That was Kendo's gameplan, but Haystacks just didn't tire out. Kendo could take anything Haystacks could throw at him in terms of being punched, but then he cracked a rib and simply couldn't go on. Haystacks tore the mask off, and Kendo covered his face and scuttled out like an animal so you never really had a good look.

Later they disqualified Haystacks because he'd taken the mask off, and you're not supposed to touch the mask. I've got that mask at home.

Giant Haystacks: The match was on and off for quite a period. Nagasaki was reluctant to wrestle me, but in the end he was forced to. Nagasaki was my most formidable opponent over the years, a very good wrestler, an opponent to be in awe of. I actually won the battle that night. He was a bit sick about it, obviously. I wasn't disqualified, no, no, no.

Lloyd Ryan: Imagine a man the size of Giant Haystacks! Forty stone! His arms are twice the size of my legs. He'd hit you on the top of the head and cave your neck in. For about a year after that match I tried to get Kendo a return with Haystacks but it never happened. And now that Nagasaki has retired it never will.

12

'I travel alone,'
said Giant Haystacks

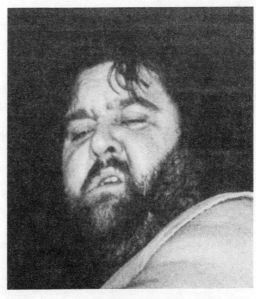

Giant Haystacks: 'He's a complex man,
much cleverer than you might think'

Max Crabtree: The big fella? Oh God, Big Luke. He's a bad'n. He's a profound liar, let's start with that. A big horrible man. I started him, but he won't tell you that. I was running the King's Hall, Belle Vue, and an old-time wrestler called Billy Graham brought him down. He was working on a club door. In those days he weighed about twenty-six stone. Looked quite tidy. Then he blew himself up, and at one time he was about forty-eight stone. A great guy, but a born liar.

Brian Dixon: Haystacks started with me very early on, before all the other big names came over. We needed a giant. I gave him the name Haystack Colhoun. I'd seen the name in an American magazine. Then we came up with Haystacks. It seemed fitting at the time.

People get sick of him, but they still come and see him. He's such a huge man – people are mesmerized by him.

Simon Garfield: The first time I saw Haystacks in the ring was in 1992 at Tunbridge Wells. He was in against Franz Schumann, a dashing Austrian thirty stones lighter.

'Wrestling,' Haystacks announced before the contest, 'is the only way to release my pent-up feelings without being prosecuted.'

I found Franz Schumann shaking gently backstage. When I asked him how he felt, he said, 'I'm confident.'

The master of ceremonies – as always at these heavyweight contests – was a tiny, weedy man in a bow-tie. He introduced Schumann as funereal music played in the background. The Austrian waved his arms in the air, as if to say, 'These are my arms. I may never use them again.'

Then Haystacks entered, to the tune of 'Two Tribes (Go To War)'. All the other wrestlers who had appeared earlier on the bill had leapt into the ring with great enthusiasm, as if to say, 'I'm ready for action!' Not Haystacks. Haystacks had a chair supplied so he could climb up and heave himself into the arena. Once there, he leaned back on the three ropes to check they could hold him.

The crowd started to shout obscenities. This angered Haystacks, and led him to complain to the referee that there was too much noise. Several minutes passed, with no wrestling. At one stage Haystacks began the complex manoeuvre that would lever his body out of the ring towards an early shower. Finally, someone with a microphone warned Haystacks that unless he started wrestling he'd be disqualified.

Haystacks then hurled himself at a startled Schumann. He lifted him up by his throat, and threw him against a corner post. After many postings, Schumann slumped to the floor and tried to crawl away. Haystacks reached outside for the timekeeper's bell, tossed it in his hands, at which point the audience started yelling 'No! No!'. Haystacks glanced at the crowd contemptuously and hit his opponent with the bell. Then I think he got too confident and turned away. The crowd cheered as Schumann arose, grabbed the bell himself and hit Haystacks on the back. Haystacks let out a slight groan. When he turned round he wasn't pleased at all.

Haystacks picked Schumann up, looked at the audience and wrapped the little Austrian in a cocoon of fear as he slammed him onto the canvas. The Austrian didn't move, and the referee counted him out. He was still lying flat out long after Haystacks had returned to his dressing room. In the end the officials rolled him under the bottom rope, and he staggered back with a blue face. Then he showered and went to the bar and told Austrian jokes.

Robbie Brookside: Haystacks can be brutal, and he'll always do enough to win, but he's not cruel. He's a complex man, much cleverer than you might think. I had a serious conversation with him about religion. It was a long car journey, and I had to keep talking so that he wouldn't fall asleep at the wheel. Normally I ask him to tell me the story of how he met Paul McCartney, which he loves, and which normally takes an hour. We've talked about South Africa and Northern Ireland. On this occasion the conversation turned to God. I mentioned that I distrusted all religion, and would rather worship a football team – they might lose, but at least you can see them. Luke took great offence. He said he was a deeply religious man, and that he wouldn't wrestle on a Sunday, and that he goes to mass whenever he can.

He used to be known as Luke McMasters. He's got about a hundred 'real names'. He likes it if I call him Louis.

Max Crabtree: Big Luke? Don't ever, *ever* travel with him. My

God . . . I know Rita well too, his wife. He's been an asset to the job. Wrestling has to have bizarre characters, it's got to have giants.

It's worth £5 just to see him try to get in the ring. When he used to wear the fur jacket and made his grand entrance . . . that was him. He earnt his money then. Now he covers himself up too much. Actually he's spoilt himself. He wants to be liked. But I said to him, 'Martin,' – that's his name, actually – 'Martin, you're a big, big fat man . . .' He was enormous. You don't see guys like him every day.

He wasn't always a nice person. He's a bit of a morose type of guy. He's on his guard all the time. Anybody who sees him in the street, the first thing they say is, 'Giant Haystacks – God, you are as fat as what I thought you were.' They always get, 'Eff-off!'

Dave Soulman Bond: I've travelled with him, and he talks about his wife and kids and his Irish background. I fought him over here and in Beirut. The bouts didn't last very long, because if he stands on you you know about it. He's a big man and he can hit you, and he can get angry. I was his tag partner a few times, and he even got angry with me then.

Once he was being interviewed by a reporter on TV, and he was asked what he liked to do in the ring most. Haystacks said, 'I like to throw people down and then bellyflop.' The reporter asked to see just the first part, and so Haystacks picked him up, and slammed him against the canvas, went 'URRRGGGHHH!!!', and the reporter just groaned and rolled off, and that was the end of the interview.

But Haystacks is a quiet guy. Gentle. He thinks a lot.

Giant Haystacks: I haven't been weighed in a while – what's the point? My weight is not a problem, not when you get used to it. I come from a family of giants; my grandfather was seven foot five. I've been wrestling since 1967, since I was thirteen. I've tried to give it up several times to concentrate on my businesses, but I've always returned when a promoter pleaded with me. I've wrestled all over the world – China, Japan, Western Samoa, Africa. High-profile people are personal friends of mine. I'm an honorary citizen of Zimbabwe, and that can open a lot of doors.

Haystacks:
'Martin,
you're a big,
big fat man'

Unknown to the public, Big Daddy and myself go to hospitals and do charity work. This year a dying child whose last wish was to come to the wrestling spent the evening with me. The following day he died.

I like to drive wherever I can. The car is my thinking place – I work it all out there, away from the wife and children. I'm a total loner. I travel alone, I wrestle alone. I look after myself. I don't need friends.

I've got a BMW and a four-wheel-drive Toyota Land Cruiser. 120,000 miles a year is nothing. I like driving to Austria for the ten-week championship, making a holiday of it, walking and fishing in the mountains between the bouts. I could fly, but these short-haul flights are the shits. I'm not comfortable on a plane, too much hassle fucking messing about, excuse the language. Short-haul there's no first class, it's all one. Not that I want to be in first class, you just get a little bit more room. I always book the seats at the back of an aircraft, I ask them to keep one spare beside me. But I always end up next to one little old lady smoking away, and she's knackered, ain't she? So then you get aggravation – 'Aren't you this Giant fellow?'

Simon Garfield: The second time I met him was in a dressing room at Croydon. He was seated, his fat folded over a sunken plastic chair, and the sweat in his beard glistened like sequins. He had just spent ten minutes pounding a smaller man against a post. He placed a towel over his legs, and began to change under it, like you see people do on the beach. He tugged off his tattered country yokel outfit, which was tight to highlight his bulk, and pulled on a loose blue tracksuit.

He said that all he was looking for was justice. This was in reference to an event many years before, the removal of British wrestling from British television in December 1988. Haystacks ran the scenario over in his head once more, but he still couldn't grasp its logic.

Giant Haystacks: What it boils down to is this. A guy called Greg Dyke took over *World of Sport* . . . he never played a sport in his life . . . he put on fucking silly darts, things like that, but he took off the wrestling. A lot of people were very disappointed. They ran opinion polls and there were ten million people who wanted wrestling back on. There's sixty million people in this country entitled to their wrestling. They are entitled to it, do you understand?

If we weren't living in such a democratic society, I'd have gone up and broke his neck. Unfortunately we've got laws of the land that don't entitle me to do that. I just don't think he had the moral right to stop all that enjoyment for so many. Instead of wrestling they put on these violent movies showing debauchery and murder. The damage to society that that does . . .

When Paul was in the Mull of Kintyre he was quite an enthusiastic artist. He'd watched me on TV, and drew me in as one of the main characters for a video. Then 20th Century Fox wanted to get involved and made a full-length film, and Paul approached me himself and said he wanted me to play a part in the movie. In the end I played two parts. The main character was called Big Bob, a character that Paul had met in the States years before, a shady record dealer, a living-on-your-wits kind of character. I played a Dickensian scene, and modern day. We were quite close, Paul and I. He would sit with me on and off the set. He used to watch the wrestling regularly. He came to see me many times when I wrestled in Sussex. He used to bring his son.

Max Crabtree: Haystacks is just a windbag. Stand on me, let's keep a spade a spade: I know the big fellow well. In the end, the ITV controller did his job, a personal thing. He decided he didn't like wrestling. That's all right. I probably don't like dog racing.

This Dyke got inundated with letters. Of course we didn't do anything to stop that. Naturally whenever we were presenting wrestling, we got the MC to say that if you're not happy that it's come off, write to this bastard. This got his back up more than ever. I had an arrangement that I used to get the ratings of how we were doing on that period on a Saturday. Our competitor was BBC *Grandstand*, and we were always a million viewers in front of it.

They scrubbed *World of Sport* first, but because wrestling was still enjoying good viewing figures, decided to keep us on. But it lost the momentum, because it would be on at one o'clock, and then at half-two. But it still didn't matter what they had on BBC, whether it was the Oxford–Cambridge boat race or a rugby union international, wrestling still had a following. But taking us off completely, well the way they did that was just too sudden.

Kent Walton's Last Commentary: Welcome, grapple fans, for the very last time. Saying goodbye is always sad, but today's sadness is eased a lot by being able to turn back the pages of wrestling's thirty-three-year history on ITV, and enjoy again some of the all-time greats. None greater, in my opinion, than the fabulous George Kidd. More of him later. Remember Oddjob? The Great Togo? Wrestling fans knew him before James Bond. Well today we can offer you the outrageous Adrian Street, Les Kellett, the tough guy who never failed to make us all laugh. Billy Two Rivers – the greatest Red Indian ring warrior of them all.

Those were the days of spectacular days at the Royal Albert Hall [screen close-up of old poster] – royal patronage, you notice, with McManus and Pallo in their heyday, and the best seats costing a princely ten guineas. Ricki Starr will parade his unique talents for us later. But notice further down the bill, a heavyweight spot featuring a rising star who really did reach the top of the pile – the late, great Mike Marino, the man who taught me so much about the ins and outs of the game. Let's enjoy him now as he faces John Kowalski from Portsmouth . . .

Johnny Kwango's trademark was his famous head-butt. Dangerous when roused, you might say. And he certainly was by Bobby Barnes, who began with his usual peacock-style display [camp shots of Barnes in a cape, frilly braces and a little Swiss Miss outfit]. We've seen those shoulder straps before, but never that front to the trunks. This is something else [bout follows, featuring a riled Kwango, who polishes his head and wins with a head-butt] . . .

Now it's back to the deep, dark ages of black and white television. Remember these opening titles? [Pallo and Kwango bounce off the ropes, with the picture occasionally frozen to show grimaces] . . .

And so I'm afraid it's goodbye to all that, grapple fans, and as I say 'have a good time' for the last time, I can't do better than to leave the final words to my good friend from Birmingham, the Giant Bomber himself, big Pat Roach:

PAT ROACH: I think today is a very, very sad day in history, that is the history of wrestling, that has been in our parlours for many many years now. How many years, Kent? Twenty?

KENT WALTON: More than that.

PAT ROACH: More than that. More than twenty years. And I feel that the wrestlers would like to say collectively, and I'm sure Caswell Martin will endorse me here now in the ring, that we are very very very sad that in the near future we will now no longer be in your front parlour.

Pat Roach: I think I spoke for all the boys. Lots of wrestlers were never great speakers. I think the fact that a wrestler was given the chance to say goodbye, rather than just an MC or an executive, I think it was rather wonderful. I credit Mike Archer for that, a TV man. It was heartfelt. I used the word parlour on purpose. I thought about it. That was the level we were at: we were welcome in anyone's parlour. Everybody loved us.

Kent Walton: Supposing you were head of sport at London Weekend Television, and you had been paying out £35,000 to put on two wrestling shows on consecutive Saturdays. The Americans come in with an hour's programme, something they've finished with, and that only costs you about £700. Which would you do?

Max Crabtree: At the end we had a new producer who wanted to get to know all about the game and get chummy with the wrestlers. Very dangerous. Previously the promoters had produced the whole show, and all the TV producer did was turn up with his cameras and film it. But this new man came in about 1987 and heard things he shouldn't. He got talking to the boys, and they started slagging people off, and some of them were downcast about the way wrestling was going. Now if you tell a TV producer that it's going downhill he's going to believe you. They told him, or he got this idea, that it was rooted in the fifties and sixties, and when Greg Dyke came round in his new job to talk to all the sports producers, our producer talked down his own job – he said it was all old-fashioned and still rooted to the sixties. Dyke took notice.

Greg Dyke: At home I've got a cartoon I bought from the *Sun* which shows me being strangled in the ring by Giant Haystacks.

When I took over the sports in 1988, ITV was losing badly in the ratings to BBC. We were stuck in about 1955, and the world had changed, and we were too downmarket. Wrestling was clearly never a proper sport – that was part of the problem. It was unfortunate really. Wrestling was unlucky, but it was so tarnished with the old-style look of ITV that it had to go. We got rid of a lot of the old game shows for the same reason. We started putting money into drama, stuff like that.

By the late 1980s the interests of the working class had changed dramatically, and we wanted to capture part of where they'd gone to, rather than where they'd been. Wrestling was stuck in a timewarp – it personified the old English working class sitting round the telly, staring blankly. That was the image we were trying to kill, so we decided to kill the wrestling.

Jackie Pallo: Why did it come off TV? Because it was crap! The young person wasn't interested any more. We lost an audience, the younger element, because it was all big fat horrible men. You don't go to see big fat horrible men. You go to see dolly fellas.

Max Crabtree: They just took it off too abruptly, killed it entirely. It was like saying, 'Right, that's it, no more football ever.' And it was still so popular at the end.

Personally it was a terrible blow, because shortly before it came off I had bought the whole thing. Whether I was set up I don't know.

Bill Abbey: Max was unfortunate. The connection with television was obviously a big part of the deal we did. I am sorry the way things worked out for him.

With wrestling, television boosted its reputation, and to some extent destroyed it. You put something on television and you go to extremes. It gobbles up the talent at an alarming rate.

Max Crabtree: After Sky started broadcasting the American wrestling I went to see the head of programmes there. This was late eighties. I took Shirley, and it was like he was my passport. The car park attendant was so thrilled to see him – 'My God, Big Daddy!' The girl on reception couldn't believe it, and started calling up her friends. The tragedy for us was the head of programmes was an Australian, and he's never seen Shirley before, never heard of Big Daddy. We went into his office and he said, 'Make it brief gentlemen – I haven't got long.' I talked about doing some British wrestling shows, and he said to go and do thirty tapes for him. I asked how much we'd get. He said same as the Americans. He put his hand up, showing five fingers. I thought he meant £5,000, but he meant £500 – £500 an hour. I worked it out. To make a tape of three forty-minute shows, with five cameras, not including Kent or paying the wrestlers, would cost £20,000. So there was clearly no way back.

13

'To my good friend Big Daddy,' wrote Margaret Thatcher

Big Daddy with Joe D'Orazio and Brian Crabtree:
'Shirley was a marvellous flagship for me'

Max Crabtree: At the end, I practically had the whole game to myself. I'd got more and more involved with Dale Martin over the years, and all the other people who were involved either retired or were bought out. So there was nothing or no one I didn't know.

There were lots of deals over the years. In the sixties Dale Martin was bought by the Hurst Park Syndicate, but kept its name and had the same people in charge. Then Jarvis Astaire, the boxing promoter, bought it. He had liked wrestling ever since he watched it as a lad at the London Ring Blackfriars. Then he bought Best Wryton Promotions, the Lancashire side of wrestling. Then of course he bought into Morrell and Beresford, which is where I am on this side of the Pennines, stretching from Leicester and Nottingham right up to Glasgow and Dundee.

Mick McManus was what we call working the pen, doing the matchmaking on behalf of Dale Martin. I knew Mick well from previous years, so he told Jarvis that I'd be the best man to revive it in the North, because it had taken a bit of a dive. When the promoters were bought out the lifeblood disappeared and they just passed it on to the secretaries. Fatal, because they knew little about it. So I took it over in the eighties and lifted it marvellously – we made very good money.

Then Mick came to see me and he said that he'd had a word with Jarvis, and that I'd done a good job, and would I take the South on as well.

Subsequently Jarvis Astaire did a deal with William Hill, and Billy Abbey got the job as deputy managing director. And so the whole thing then belonged to the public company, and I was running the wrestling scene on William Hill's behalf, the whole thing including the television.

It was clear that William Hill no longer wanted to keep wrestling as part of the bookmaking business, because it had nothing to do with bookmaking. It was the one thing you couldn't put a bet on, a bit of an embarrassment to them really. So I bought it all out, in 1986 I think.

It was in my interest to make new stars, as many as I could. The problem with some of the wrestlers was they had quite a lot of talent, but they had no style. But even before television, my brother Shirley was always a main event man.

There was no doubt that there were certain personalities that captured the public's imagination, and Big Daddy . . . well if you saw in my brother's house, the pictures that he had: people like Margaret Thatcher and Lord Havers, the Attorney General, you'd be amazed who actually used to watch us.

My brother was invited by the *Daily Star* to go to the Inn on the Park, Park Lane. He was just one of the guests, there were about five hundred showbusiness personalities there. At that time the *Daily Star* had been very kind to him. He'd been doing Father Christmas and went round the kids' hospitals. He was a great figure for the kids – he was nice with them. Any road, they were going to give him a Gold Star award.

The guest speaker was Margaret Thatcher. My brother Shirley was sat at a table with Jeremy Beadle on one side of him, and various others. This guy came over to him and said, 'Hallo Shirley, how you keeping?' Nobody ever called my brother Shirley except them that knew him well. The fellow said, 'You don't know who I am,' and Shirley said, 'No, sorry, I don't.'

The man said, 'I am Mrs Thatcher's press secretary, Bernard Ingham. I know you well, Shirley. I used to watch you wrestle at the Drill Hall in Halifax. I've told Mrs Thatcher about you, and she's dying to meet you. She's watched you many times on telly.'

Shirley says, 'I'd be delighted.' Lo and behold, she does her speech, walks across the floor, doesn't say hello to any of the other stars there, comes over to the table. Shirley stands up, and she holds his hand very warmly and says, 'I've been dying to meet you. I'm a great fan. I must tell you, Bernard and I have just come back from Kenya, and after we'd done the formalities we went to a state banquet. I sat down with the minister to have a meal, and the first question they asked me was, 'Do you know the wrestler Big Daddy?' Naturally Bernard said, "Of course, of course." Apparently you're a household name in Africa.'

Mrs Thatcher then said, 'Would you be able to send me half a dozen signed photographs down to Downing Street?'

Shirley was more than pleased.

She sent him the most beautiful letter back, a beautiful portrait of herself: 'To my good friend Big Daddy, Margaret Thatcher'.

You see, Thames International sold wrestling all over the world. Of course these African countries didn't want to see *Coronation Street*, but wrestling rang a bell. Shirley met Princess Margaret at the Children's Royal Variety Performance. They all had to line up in the foyer after the show, and she was moving along the opposite side to where Shirley was but she came across especially to talk to him. It wasn't his turn. She got her hand out and she said, 'Big Daddy, I've been wanting to meet you for a long time. My sister watches you on television. When you walked on that stage earlier it was like magic.' They had all sorts there – Geoff Capes, Ian Botham, but they were all in blazers, and for children it didn't mean anything. But when Shirley came on in his shimmering thing . . . he was the kids' hero.

Shirley was in the Coldstream Guards for a short stint, and he brought his busby out with him. So when he went back in the ring in the seventies after his short retirement we brought him back as the Battling Guardsman, a villain. He used to come into the ring to Joseph Locke's 'Soldier's Dream', apart from the time when the idiot in the control room put on the other side, 'The Oldest City'.

I'd say that the Big Daddy thing was my idea. I'd been to see the film of Tennessee Williams's *Cat on a Hot Tin Roof*, and in that Burl Ives plays Big Daddy. At this point Shirley was in the *Guinness Book of Records* as having the biggest chest in Great Britain. It was sixty-four inches. I said to him, 'I think we'll leave the Guardsman out and we'll try Big Daddy,' and it just clicked. This was in the late seventies. He invested in the right clothes, the top hat and that, and people went mad. Now we wanted some music that was out of copyright, and we found out that 'We Shall Not Be Moved' was an old American folk song. It just matched what we were looking for, and so Shirley was launched.

It just hit home. The photos on his wall with Kenneth Newman the police commissioner, Tommy Cooper of course, all of them . . .

Kent Walton loves to tell this story about a letter he got from a woman viewer. She said she'd always been a Big Daddy fan, but often wondered how he got that name for his move, the Big Daddy

Daddy on *Tiswas*: 'Big Daddy was the first thing that started killing wrestling'

Splash. She wrote, 'I was coming home from a holiday in Cornwall with my family, and we pulled up at a service station. It's about two in the morning, and there was a car next to us filling up. All of a sudden Big Daddy gets out, and goes to the back of the car and urinates. I was going to ask him for his autograph, but he was still urinating several minutes later. Now I know where the expression the Big Splash comes from.'

Shirley did *Surprise Surprise* with Cilla, about his lifeguard days, and then *This Is Your Life*. A complete surprise. He thought he was going to a photocall for the *TV Times*. Eamonn Andrews came on as a masked man. After the show, which went out live at seven, they drove him in a fast car to go top of the bill at Leicester De Montfort Hall.

Brian Crabtree: Shirley would get asked to do crazy things. People would come up and say, 'Can you hold my little baby son up on one finger, and we'll take the photograph?' Shirley would go, 'Don't be so daft. The child will be frightened to death.' So he'd just stand with them side by side and take a nice photo that way.

Max Crabtree: I almost cry when I think of some of those houses I went to with Shirley where there were kids dying. Never mind about his critics – he didn't *have* to do it. He'd pick them up in his arms and it would choke me because I had five sons of my own. There was a little boy who was on his last hurrah, and his little eyes when he saw Shirley come in . . . Shirley took him his top hat and a load of nice pictures he had and a scarf.

Dave Soulman Bond: The Big Daddy era was a turning point. I'm not saying Daddy wasn't a good wrestler – the crowd loved him, he put arses on seats – it's just that he wasn't really a *technician*. It began a downward trend then. The first couple of years of Daddy was okay, but after that . . .

I fought Daddy several times. Fairfield Halls, Hanley, all over the place. He's got smelly armpits. But it's exciting, because before you even walk out into the ring the atmosphere that he used to generate gets your adrenalin going. But because of the weight difference you couldn't really wrestle him properly.

But he was fit. I'll give him his due – he did use to do a bit of training, and I went to the gym with him in Crystal Palace when he was in London. But when he got in the ring, you couldn't do a lot with him.

I wasn't frightened. With the big fellows, their objective is not to maim, whatever the public may think. The public get it wrong – they see certain moves and they think, Christ, that guy should be maimed, but that is not the objective. Even Daddy understood that

Daddy meets
Princess Margaret:
'My sister watches
you on television'

we were all doing it for a living. You don't fear your opponent. I never show a lot of respect for my opponent, but I never underestimated him. I never beat him either, solo or tag. Daddy won, and that was it, and I could never stamp my authority on him.

Adrian Street: Max brought Shirley back. He told me he'd been living on the dole for years. Max is the one with the imagination, but the worst bit of imagination he ever had was creating a new character for Shirley, because Big Daddy was the thing that started killing wrestling. You can't blame the imported American TV wrestling shows for taking the British wrestling off TV. That was down to Shirley.

Max started picking his opponents, and the only people he didn't ask to do it were people like me who had too much pride. All of a sudden all these stars who hadn't been beaten for years were suddenly being beaten in two minutes. If it had taken him three minutes to beat them he probably would have died of a heart attack. He'd blow up walking to the ring. If you push him on his arse he'd make himself sick trying to get up. The worst thing that ever happened to British wrestling.

With Daddy it was the same thing every time: he'd be on with a light tag team partner of 150 pounds, and this chap would get mangled by their opponents who would be 300 pounders. But at the last minute Big Daddy would come to the rescue, and the trumpets would go ta-ra-ta-ra, and it would be all over. How dumb do they think people are?

When Max took charge of Joint Promotions I would say that he purposely tried to run the business down. I think he might have had the idea of running the business down and then buying it from Jarvis Astaire, buying it for peanuts and then building it back up again. I think he was quite clever and I've always respected Max, which is why I'm always suspicious about how badly the whole thing went.

He thought he could build it up again just with Shirley, but Shirley killed too many dragons, too many ogres, too many guys that really meant something, and the business can't survive without its heels. The success of a wrestling territory is only defined by the success of its heels.

Max Crabtree: Shirley's thing was being a big man. With Daddy, he was too big to wrestle like a ten-stone man, darting about the ring. Using his belly, checking people, his Splash – that was his style, same as Haystacks. Eight minutes, in and out. There was a time when promoters used to insist that all wrestlers do a certain amount of wrestling in the ring, at least twenty minutes, and it was bloody awful. People used to sit there yawning. You don't want to see Shirley spend fifteen minutes putting on a leglock.

Mal Sanders: I was Daddy's tag partner for a while. You can't blame Daddy for what happened. I have to say that Max Crabtree never did me any harm at all. Daddy's *This Is Your Life* was a great day. All the boys were there. Mick came on . . . Anita Harris . . . some girl whose life he had saved after talking to her when she was in a coma.

There was a tag match at Croydon between Big Daddy and Steve Grey on one side, and Banger Walsh and the Bulk. It got to the point when Banger Walsh had slammed Stevie Grey, and all the Bulk had to do in this match was get in and splash him. Unfortunately, the Bulk wore dungarees, with a bib and braces, and during the course of the match one of his straps had come undone and the referee had ordered him to clip it up. Unintentionally the Bulk had done his strap up over the top rope, so the rope was actually inside the dungaree. When the big finish came, Banger Walsh tagged him, and he kept trying to get in, but he just didn't manage it. He couldn't work out what was holding him back. And there was only a limited amount of time that Steve Grey could stay on the floor.

Max Crabtree: All the time with wrestling one of the hardest things was when wrestlers felt they had something to tell the world, something sensational. And of course newspapers don't want to hear the other side of it, the reasons, the business. They just want the exposé. Wrestling was on the newspaper hit-list, although some way below royalty and politicians. Down at about number thirty. But every now and then the papers did like a bit of wrestling scandal. Most of it was born out of jealousy, wishing they might have been something they weren't.

Tony Banger Walsh, the *Sun*, 1985: Big Daddy used me as a fight fall-guy. The whole thing is more of a show than a scrap. Some of the top wrestlers couldn't fight their way out of a wet paper bag. Big Daddy gets all the glory but I wouldn't fancy his chances in a genuine, no-holds-barred match. The worst thing is the way he has become a kiddies' folk hero. That made me want to throw up, because when he's not in the limelight he doesn't treat kids as extra special.

Max Crabtree: In the army they say that there's a field marshal's baton in everyone's bag. All wrestlers believed that they could have been stars. They can't. It's one of those unusual situations: there's something missing. But they shoot eagles, not sparrows. The ones who criticized Shirley were the sparrows.

Big Daddy: The most hurtful thing was what he said about me and kids. I love children and everyone who knows me is well aware of that.

Max Crabtree: What really hit us hard was Mal Kirk's death. What happened to Mal could have happened to anybody, but Mal was well overweight, a mighty man. Let's not kid ourselves: Mal's life was that of working club doors. He'd do club jobs that most men would have run a mile from. He spent his life in physical things. Mal played rugby opposite Shirley when they were teenagers. We all knew Mal well.

It was at the Hippodrome Great Yarmouth, the main event tag match, the match before the intermission. Shirley body-checked him, Mal went down and Shirley dropped down across him, the

Mal King Kong Kirk:
'I don't want to go.
I hate this job'

Splash. Took the winning fall. Shirley got up, the crowd were ecstatic. A holiday crowd all around the ring.

Mal was still on the floor. Most wrestlers after a fall would either get to their feet or roll under the bottom rope out of the ring. But you could see something was wrong. Shirley tells the second, I see it and run to the ring, and of course Mal was in the early process of dying. He was going purple.

It was in the circus arena, and many of those people used to love the wrestling. The head of a Slavonic pole act was watching. He got in the ring, and he knew what was happening too. We were trying to work his chest, and the ambulance men tried. The problem was the poor man had died in the ring. He had such an enormous girth, about twenty-five stone, and we couldn't get him out. We had to take the ropes down. He was announced dead on arrival at the hospital.

Shirley was devastated, and we had to go to the police station, and then it was the most depressing journey back home. It was Sunday night, dawn breaking, a gloomy morning at about five o'clock, and we were coming over that stretch from King's Lynn towards Newark, from the Norfolk Broads. I had to call his wife Ilona.

Ilona was his second wife. They met in Germany at one of the tournaments. He gave her a couple of kids, and they lived amongst miners on an old housing estate in Castleford. Poor Ilona.

Ilona Kirk: I feel very bitter. Mal's job depended on making Big Daddy good in the ring. He was always the shaven-headed baddie while Big Daddy was the kiddies' favourite. But in reality Mal was honest, decent and kind-hearted.

Mal was paid only £25 a night for being hurled all over the canvas. But if he fought Big Daddy he got an extra £5. We were glad of the money, so Mal went to Yarmouth even though it meant a ten-hour round trip. Mal was in the process of pulling out of the fight game because of the lousy money and long hours and had made inquiries about managing a pub. His last words to me before he left the house were, 'I don't want to go. I hate this job.'

*

Max Crabtree: Shirley was a marvellous flagship for me, but he's totally finished now. He's been out a while. I told him, 'You'd better get out.' Because whatever people say about it, you've got to take chances and you do get bumps. Unfortunately, two or three years ago he was in the ring at Hornsey and got caught with a bad bang on the side of the head and it formed a type of paralysis. We had a flask of tea in the car on the way back, and Shirley couldn't hold it up. So he went to see a specialist and was told the worse. It's now affected his walking, given him a slight limp.

He still has his own gym, and his own wrestling dummy, a leather one specially made for the Olympic wrestlers. He has one

Daddy holds kids: 'Never mind about his critics – he didn't *have* to do it'

about fifteen stone. They're the same size as a man, and he throws them up and down.

He'll go in the gym every day. He likes boxing, and he watches Sky, a marvellous variation from the other channels. He goes to the coast a lot – he likes Blackpool, believe it or not. It's the air he likes. He doesn't smoke, doesn't drink, never has. He always did like the wrestling.

14

'And now my dad drives my Jag,' said the British Bulldog

British Bulldog: 'I talk to dying kids'

Jackie Pallo Junior: The main problem was that we'd forgotten how to make it exciting. The American scene was entirely different. Our guys, like the Big Daddys, were these grotesque guys in diapers, but in America you had these wrestling Arnold Schwarzenegger types, these Hollywood blonds – very, very good looking. They were only doing their two or three minutes, and had obviously worked out their routines, but they were capturing a new audience, the kids, a very, very lucrative market.

Simon Garfield: I first saw the Americans wrestle in 1992, at its peak or just past it, with 20,000 others at Madison Square Garden. Hulk Hogan was on show, the master of merchandise. There seemed to be about three hundred Hulk-endorsed products on sale, including vitamins, cookies and deodorant. It was an afternoon show, and half the audience were under sixteen, yelling things like 'Snap his neck!' and 'Choke him!' The wildest reaction came from the cheapest seats. Wrestling is funny that way: the further away you are, the better it looks.

As well as Hulk there was the Undertaker, escorted into the ring by his manager, Paul Bearer. There was 'Tax Inspector' Irwin R Shyster (IRS), who wore a shirt and tie, and there was Davey Boy Smith, born near Wigan, appearing in Union Jack Spandex as the British Bulldog. There was also someone called Berserker, a bearded, slightly trimmer version of Giant Haystacks, with none of Haystacks's grandeur. He spent much of his match crawling around on his hands and knees, slobbering at his opponent's legs. For this he was paid hundreds of dollars a night. His agent boasted how no one could drool like Berserker.

The climax was a twenty-man battle royal, with all the wrestlers in the ring at once, all trying to avoid being thrown over the top rope. The last man standing won. After twenty minutes there were two men left, Sid Justice and Hulk Hogan, who was always expected to win. Hulk then hurled Justice over to huge cheers, but in so doing also knocked out the referee, thus rendering him unable to declare the winner. Justice then crawled back and, with the referee still out, threw Hogan through the middle rope, an illegal move. The referee came to, saw Justice alone in the ring and declared him the victor. The crowd went mad and ripped up their foam Undertaker tombstones and threw shoes into the ring.

Bobby Heenan: I've been in wrestling here for more than twenty years, used to wrestle before the commentating. And I've formed a philosophy about it: the idea is to make as much as you can as quick as you can as easy as you can. You only get one shot at life. If people don't like you, that's tough. When I go to deposit at my bank in Beverly Hills and the cashier says, 'Thank you,' that's all I care about.

Ten years ago I thought the business was as big as you could get. The music and the merchandising has gone wild. The athletes are getting quicker and bigger. When I started, a 250-pound guy was big. Now a 300-pound guy is only average. You have the National Disasters – they're close to 500 pounds, and quick. André the Giant, he's over 500 pounds, and he's got a little bit of a bad knee, but he's still like a guided missile.

People demand action and glamour. If you'd took all the jewellery off Liberace, he'd have been just another piano player. You put all that stuff on to attract attention to yourself, and without it you're just another athlete.

Brian Howard Finkelman: I work in the talent relations department and I'm a technical adviser on the WWF magazine. I've been a wrestling fan for thirty years. I've been with WWF for fifteen years. It's a pleasure to be associated with the World Wrestling Federation.

The big change started happening in 1984. Prior to that, wrestling was a territorial thing, and the WWF was a north-eastern organization. When Vince decided to expand in 1984 and go national, that was the start of it all. And it hasn't stopped yet!

Before 1984 you would still have seen a good card, but lacking probably a lot of the entertainment value you now have, namely the glitz, the glamour, the glitter, the fireworks, the talent, the moves that the talent makes. Everything has progressed, and it's progressed to the better.

Vince McMahon dares to be different. When Vince decided he was in the driving seat, things started happening.

Things began peaking in the late eighties, that's when Hulk Hogan was at his height. Hulk was the man. Hulkamania was one of the greatest phenomenons in sports entertainment. You thought WWF, you thought Hulk. You thought Hulk, you thought WWF. It was a triangle. WWF plus fans equals Hulk. Hulk plus fans equals WWF. That's the way I view it.

There's a slogan: 'Where we going? I don't know where we're going, but we're on our way.' And that's the way I felt back then.

We never believed in that slogan, 'If it ain't broke don't fix it.' A lot of things never broke, but we were always fixing. We always stayed one step ahead, never satisfied, always looking for new product, to continue to instil new ideas, new creativity, new talent, new attitudes, because that keeps your product fresh and gives you a better product to offer your public.

New York Times, **20 June 1991:** Hulk Hogan and Rowdy Roddy Piper are among five professionals from the World Wrestling Federation who are scheduled to testify that they bought anabolic steroids from Dr George T Zahorian in a trial that begins here Monday.

Zahorian, a 43-year-old osteopath and urologic surgeon, faces 15 counts of illegally distributing steroids and controlled substances to wrestlers and weight lifters nationwide.

Hogan, whose real name is Terry Bollea, and Piper, whose real name is Roderick Toomba, will be joined by Richard Vigneoult, known professionally as Rick Martel, plus Brian Blair and Daniel Stivey. In an attempt to protect Hogan's reputation, his attorney is attempting to persuade the United States attorney's office to allow him not to testify.

'I can tell you that the use of steroids is not limited to these wrestlers, but that they are used throughout the World Wrestling Federation,' William C Costapoulos, defense attorney, said. 'The demands are heavy that they use them from the WWF. They either use them or they don't participate.'

Brian Howard Finkelman: What the competition does is what we've done. They do what we did. Do you follow me? We do, and they follow, that's the way I've always maintained it. We provide an evening you'll never forget. The fans grow up, you've got them and you hope you never lose them. I was talking to some fans on our computer service online, and they first got into it when they were seven or eight and now they're seventeen. We cater to kids a lot, they love our product, and we want to nurture them that way. So then they move into the new cycle with the new children.

The talent to look for now is Shawn Michaels, the 123 Kid, a kid with attitude. Skip's potential is endless, and certainly there's Bret Hart, our champion. His future can only be as good as he wants it to be. Hunter Hearst Helmsley I think has a great future. He's going to be moving along very nicely as we move along.

New York Times, 24 June 1991: Assistant United States attorney Theodore Smith asserted today that a suburban Harrisburg doctor acted as a drug dealer, not a physician, by selling anabolic steroids to professional wrestlers.

Smith said four of the steroid counts are based on delivery to Rick Martel, Daniel Stivey, Brian Blair and Roddy Piper. A fifth count, providing steroids to World Wrestling Federation champion Hulk Hogan, was dropped after United States District Court Judge William Caldwell ruled Hogan did not have to honor a subpoena to testify because of 'private and personal matters that should be protected'.

'If anybody has any illusions about professional wrestling being a pure sport,' Smith said in his opening argument, 'we may burst your bubble.'

Shawn Michaels: What I do is certainly not like the old English stuff, because the old stuff is boring. People are always going to pass judgement on things they know absolutely nothing about. That's something we understand: when you're on top, everybody's going to take shots at you, and then years later they're going to call you the greatest. Just like they did with Muhammad Ali. Who, as we all know, learnt all he knew about self-promotion, and talking himself up before a fight, from wrestling.

Every big guy in the gym thinks he can become a wrestler. I'm not the biggest guy, but the fact of the matter is I'm a damn good athlete, probably the best in the wrestling business. I'm twenty-nine

Shawn Michaels:
'I've eaten more chicken than any man should'

Dynamite Kid:
'Tommy's a broken man'

Hunter Hearst Helmsley:
'I'm not in this business for my fans'

years old. I work hard – I train about ninety minutes a day, both weights and aerobic training. A strict diet. I eat a lot of high-protein, moderate carbohydrates, no fat, exclusively egg whites in the morning. I haven't had a fried egg or a poached egg or a yellow egg in ten years. I eat about eight to ten scrambled egg whites every morning, maybe with a bowl of oatmeal or a bagel or two, and after I eat grilled chicken. I've eaten more chicken than any man should. It's not an exciting diet. A lot of dry pasta.

If you personally wanted to become a wrestler, Simon, looking at you I can tell you would need a complete genetic change, a complete transplant and transfusion of DNA. Some people are born big, some people are born this way or that way, and you're born like that. It's just unfortunate. God gives everyone their special gift, and I guess your gift lies elsewhere.

I work 365 days a year. It's gruelling. I was being raised to be a lineback at football. But the first night I got to stay up late at the age of twelve, I watched wrestling on TV. The first time I saw it I was hooked. I was hungry. It's just one of those things that make you believe in fate and destiny. The minute I saw it I knew. I could never get it out of my mind.

When everyone asked on graduation day what I wanted to become, and everyone else was saying 'a doctor' or 'join the airforce', I said I wanted to become a professional wrestler. They joked, but now look, I'm the best, and they're ordinary. Good luck to them, but will they ever earn what I do, have fans shout 'Pretty Boy!!' at them like I do? I don't think so. I very much doubt it.

I started training when I was eighteen, and I had my first match a couple of weeks after my nineteenth birthday. Ten years and I'm still learning. At the beginning I got beat up and lost a lot. It's like your mum and your dad – they tell you things as a child and you disagree and say they're not right, but nothing speaks louder than experience. But my parents were right: everything I needed to know I learnt at kindergarten – yes and no, right from wrong, black from white. With a little dedication, good things come. It sounds very old fashioned, but it's a fact.

The worst thing about wrestling is the same thing that's exciting about it – the travel. Being away from the people you love, the people that you want to give to, and the people that you'd like to get to know.

Then there's accidents. Everyone says wrestling is fake, but it's very much real. It's exactly what you see. That's something that people never get over. They always say, 'How did you do that without hurting?' Well we don't. If it looks like it hurts, the chances are pretty good that it hurts. It's very simple.

In the eighties society is what changed wrestling. Society demanded more. Wrestling adapted, created more colourful characters, involved the audience more in their sport. With the World Wrestling Federation we are catering to everyone. We want mums and dads to bring their children and feel comfortable and to know that their children will not walk out of there with anything that's negative. They're not going to see gore, or have bad use of language, it's a healthy atmosphere. The World Wrestling Federation is trying to make a statement, trying to stand for what's good, do something decent for society. I realize the press likes to make fun and dig dirt, but face it: when all the fun's been made, and all the press are old and grey, the World Wrestling Federation is still going to be here. We have a standard by which we're going to live our lives and do our job. Our fans are loyal and we're loyal to them.

I think the next step for me is broadcasting and production behind the scenes, other fields of entertainment. When people don't want to see me any more I'm going to move on and I want to be one of the very few people in the World Wrestling Federation to bow out gracefully and I'll not be bitter.

When I go back we're inducting some older wrestlers into the Hall of Fame – the second year. There's a big dinner in Philadelphia. I believe that the Wrestling Hall of Fame will be in Baltimore. It's just our way of trying to say thanks to some people.

Vince McMahon: Unlike my trailblazing family predecessors, I began to promote the WWF not as sport but as family-orientated sports entertainment. With this new positioning came an avalanche of even greater popularity. We began to attract more charismatic performers. We began to license their likenesses on products the world over. More and more, we began to earn the respect, trust and admiration of legions of fans.

Anyone in any country can understand wrestling. There is no rule book to master. It is as comprehensible in China as it is in Canada. Children love it. Our guys are role models for kids every-where. These are guys you can take home to Mom – even Mama-san in Japan or Mumsie in England.

Our performers became stars, our stars became superstars, our superstars became superheroes. With this status came an unprece-dented responsibility. We accepted the responsibility to set for our-selves and for our athletes the highest moral and ethical standards.

New York Times, **28 June 1991:** A doctor was convicted yesterday by a Federal jury in Harrisburg, Pa, of selling anabolic steroids and controlled substances to four professional wrestlers and a weightlifter. George T Zahorian was convicted on 12 counts. He faces up to 44 years in jail and a $3m fine.

Max Crabtree: The Americans – do not be under any illusions. That is the sick part of it. I couldn't believe it when I've seen the state of these buggers when they go in the ring. This bodybuilding . . . that side of wrestling is terrible. They're involved in these sup-plements and they're dangerous. And I read where they take them from, out of dead bodies, their kidneys for the testosterone. They inject it into them. They get it from these Third World countries where life is cheap. I've brought Americans over to this country for years, and the first time I experienced it . . . we had one guy at the Albert Hall who was running with his head into the wall of the dressing room.

Vince McMahon: In June 1987, on our own initiative, the WWF began a substance abuse programme that called for weekly, random drug testing of all our athletes. In the last year alone more than 2,500 such tests were administered in more than one hundred cities nationwide. Those athletes who tested positive were immediately suspended for six weeks without pay. Second offenders had to complete an accredited rehabilitation programme. A third offence results in termination. When the rehabilitated athlete returns to the ring, his share of the rehabilitation cost is deducted from his next twenty-six paycheques. This method of repayment serves as a constant reminder of his breach of public trust.

New York Times, **12 July 1994:** A former wrestler testified in Federal court today that Vincent K McMahon, the wrestling promoter, personally asked him to use steroids.

The testimony, by Kevin Patrick Wacholz, whose professional wrestling persona was a convict called Nailz, came after three days of more general testimony about the use of anabolic steroids by Hulk Hogan and other professional wrestlers. It was the first testimony directly linking Mr McMahon to steroid use.

Mr Wacholz claimed that during a conversation in January 1992, Mr McMahon told him that at 200lbs he was still not big enough to portray the Nailz character. Mr Wacholz testified that he told Mr McMahon he had been working out regularly but not taking steroids and that Mr McMahon responded 'You should be.'

'I strongly suggest you go on the gas,' he said Mr McMahon told him. Earlier, the prosecutor had established that 'gas' is sometimes used as a slang term for steroids.

Dr George T Zahorian also testified that Mr McMahon was a customer for steroids. Dr Zahorian testified that Emily Feinberg, then Mr McMahon's executive secretary, 'would contact me, contact my office, speak to me personally, and ask if I would send up the anabolic steroids to Mr McMahon's office, up to Titan Sports'.

A lawyer for Mr McMahon sought to establish from Dr Zahorian that these steroids were for Mr McMahon's personal use as an amateur bodybuilder and not for distribution to wrestlers.

New York Times, 15 July 1994: Hulk Hogan (Terry Gene Bollea) said that while touring for the World Wrestling Federation, he would call Emily Feinberg 'and ask her to place an order for me with Dr Zahorian'.

Mr Bollea, who now wrestles on a rival circuit, Ted Turner's Atlanta-based World Championship Wrestling, said that when the steroid orders arrived at Titan Sports headquarters, he would 'pick them up along with my paycheck, fan mail or whatever'. He also said that Mr McMahon never ordered him to take steroids and never purchased any steroids for him.

New York Times, 23 July 1994: Vincent K McMahon, who brought professional wrestling into the entertainment mainstream, was acquitted today by a jury in Federal District Court of charges that he conspired to distribute steroids to his wrestlers.

In a news conference outside the courthouse, Mr McMahon said his wrestling promotion concern survived the sort of scrutiny few corporations undergo.

'The World Wrestling Federation is about fun,' he said. 'It's not about courtrooms.'

Simon Garfield: I went to see the Americans again in 1995, in Hershey, Pennsylvania, where the chocolate comes from, a big WWF 'In Your House' live pay-per-view, a monthly event. There were seven thousand in the audience, and the PR man said they had over two hundred thousand subscribers watching all over the country at $19.95 a time.

The main events were the British Bulldog against his brother-in-law Bret Hitman Hart, and the Undertaker versus King Mabel in what they called a 'casket match' (the loser being carried away in a coffin).

The talent arrived at the indoor arena throughout the afternoon. Most had travelled on the WWF bus, but some made their own way with their families. They seemed to get on well, high-fiving, eating together in the makeshift canteen, pasta, burgers, brownies, as they watched the football game and shouted at the little screen in the corner of the room.

Backstage, the wrestlers were treated like artists, not roughhouse pugilists. WWF management wondered whether they would be so kind to do this, whether that might be at all possible. Most wrestlers were on short-term contracts, and could defect to rivals if they failed to get the respect, wages or exposure they felt they deserved.

The one place they could not go was the Ultimate Fighting Championship, the latest American attempt to sate a public hunger for more violence and more blood. Unlike pro wrestling, the UFC presented 'real' fighting inside a large octagonal meshed cage. Competitors could do anything they wished to gain victory over an opponent, bar biting and eye-gouging. In UFC there are no recognized moves, no pins, no tricky aerial manoeuvres off top ropes. There are no flamboyant costumes, and no plots. As proof of its credentials, and to confound cynics who still suspect fakery, fans may bet on the outcome of a fight. The winner is usually the one left standing, but even he may end the evening in the emergency room. Congressmen have not been slow in trying to ban it from their states, frightened by the growing popularity it commands.

Predictably, the World Wrestling Federation disapproves of the UFC, comparing it to licensed human cockfighting. The WWF could have gone that way in the early eighties, it contends, but chose to reject barbarism and embrace the family. Merchandising potential had something to do with this too.

The WWF stars began getting ready at about six, changing on their own first, and then joining a production line of make-up, costume repairs and pumped-up television interviews (during which they said improbable things like 'I'm gonna rip his arse right out of its socket!'). Then they planned their matches with opponents and referees, and maybe visited Vince McMahon's office for a pep talk. The Undertaker strolled around in cheery mood. Davey Boy Smith, the British Bulldog, again told people how he got his middle name ('The clerk at the register office was in a rush – filled in the first name section with David, but should have put 'Boy' in the next column, where it asked for sex'). Then there were some new figures, Golddust, the Smoking Gunns and Hunter Hearst Helmsley, who wore white gloves and carried a cane.

Hunter Hearst Helmsley: Hunter Hearst Helmsley is superior to the other wrestlers in the World Wrestling Federation through the simple fact of breeding. I come from the finest family, a rich history of great people. My background allowed me to have the best personal trainers to become a professional wrestler, and my education in the finest schools in the world allowed me to be smarter than everybody else here. I have the total package.

I fight in this business for honour, glory and splendour, not for the money. I don't really care about my fans, I'm not in this business for them. The one thing they'll do after they watch me in the ring is respect me. When I first came into wrestling people felt I was just a rich and prissy aristocrat, and they didn't take my challenge seriously. I was just some priss. But as time has gone on, they have seen that I'm a serious threat, and anyone who has stepped into the ring with me thinks I'm the best athlete in the world today. The World Wrestling Federation is where everybody wants to be. Are any of the other athletes here as great as me? No they are not. My goal is the heavyweight championship. When I want it, it will be mine. Soon the title shots will come my way and you will see plenty of gold around Hunter Hearst Helmsley's waist. This is the big dance.

Simon Garfield: He then went on to wrestle a man called Henry O Godwin, a lowlife backwoodsman, in 'an Arkansas hogpen match', a bout that began in the ring, but ended in a scrap amongst seven pigs in an adjacent enclosure. The pigs squealed as the two men covered themselves in porcine faeces.

Davey Boy Smith: I was so skinny – people don't believe me when I tell them now.

I'm from Golbourne, the other side of Wigan. When I was about twelve, my cousin was wrestling for the Crabtrees, and my parents wanted to get me into something that would keep me off the streets. I started amateur first. I was watching Steve Logan, Big Daddy, Mick McManus, Adrian Street, all at the Blackpool Tower. To pay for my tuition I had to deliver fruit on my bike, on the handlebars. They wouldn't let me write down the delivery orders. I had to memorize them all, just like you have to do in the ring, I had to memorize all the moves. That's why my memory's really good.

When I was fifteen I was told that I was wrestling professionally against Bernie Wright. I said, 'In the gym?'

'No, Solihull.'

I think it was the same week that Elvis Presley died. Big Daddy was on the card. No matter where I went Big Daddy was on the card. It would always sell out. I was the smallest wrestler they had. I couldn't have been 140 pounds sopping wet. The guys used to tease me all the time. I was thin, but really fit. I could wrestle for two hours straight, no problem. But the teasing used to upset me, so I kept a list on paper of all the guys who did it. And you know what? When I go home, I never have the time of day for them. When those wrestlers come to see me now, I go, 'I remember you.'

Max Crabtree: When Davey Boy first came to see me he wasn't like now – now he's nineteen and a half stone. Normally when new guys came in, if they had to duck their heads when they came through the door I always thought I could get them work. But Davey was what we used to call pencil-necked. Yet he was so eager. I paired him with my brother Shirley.

Davey Boy Smith: I was Big Daddy's tag team partner for a while, when I was still at school. You turned the TV on, and there I was. Young David Smith. I was getting the beatings, I was getting beatings so good that the people were almost crying, 'That poor little helpless boy!' Then when I tagged Big Daddy he came in and cleaned up. We were selling out everywhere. So I went to school the next Monday, having been on TV, and – boom! – instant respect from the teachers. They all said, 'Oh, he knows where he's going.' But I kept on with my school, and with rugby. I tried out for Wigan on the wing. So fast. And now . . . If Daddy hadn't had the stroke we could still do the same thing over again. But he's a little bit old now, a little bit bitter some people would say.

After England it all began in Japan, and then I got the call from WWF who liked my style, all this high-flying stuff. I began with the Dynamite Kid, my cousin, and the British Bulldogs tag team just knocked them out.

Max Crabtree: The Dynamite Kid was the one, a great wrestler. He was brought to me from the Isle of Man. He was an introvert, but the minute he got in the ring he changed immediately. No verbals, but physical, a lot of steam. His name was Tommy Billington.

He was doing well for me, but then he announced that he was going to Canada, Calgary, the next day to go work with the Harts. I knew Stu Hart well. He had about nine children, including Bret and Owen who I brought over to fight over here.

Stu was very friendly with Vince McMahon, and so Tommy had a great introduction. He did well in Canada, and then great for Vince, built himself up with weights and later, when his cousin came over, they formed the British Bulldogs. His cousin was Davey Boy. Very few English had ever cracked it in the States, but they were the exception. A huge hit. They had a bulldog called Matilda that came in the ring with them.

Tommy got badly injured, hurt his back. He also fell out very badly with Vince – too much of a maverick. Tried to nail an opponent's boots to the floor, silly stuff, stuff you don't do. Davey Boy is still big over there, but Tommy's a broken man. He hates Davey Boy.

Diana Hart: We met in May 1981 when he first came to Calgary. I saw his picture in the programme, the young star. He had a bite on his arm from a trip to South Africa, and I got to meet him and he asked me for a plaster. I was fascinated by him. Up until then I think my mum and dad were concerned that I hadn't had any interest in men. When I saw him wrestle he was like no one else I had ever seen before. I had a really hard time forgetting about him. We got married in '84.

Davey Boy Smith: Things weren't always going so great for me here. I fell out with the WWF in 1992. I left, and they wanted to keep my name, the British Bulldog. But I had already trademarked it, so they couldn't touch me. I said they could use it for merchandising for two years. But then I came back, and now I'm getting title shots.

Simon Garfield: His fight with his brother-in-law was one of the most aggressive I'd seen, twenty minutes of muscled stunts that left both fighters drained. Bret Hitman Hart, the victor, needed stitches in his back.

The crowd loathed Smith's new style. He used to be clean, but he 'turned bad' to get more attention. Fifteen minutes after the bout, still short of breath, he said how pleased he was with the audience reaction, but he was coming down fast. He said that tomorrow it was Newark, Delaware.

Davey Boy Smith: I miss my parents and the food. My parents are alive still, in the same house I was born. And now my dad drives my Jag, the one I had from my last British tour, and he really enjoys it.

Now when I come in to England, the customs guys all know me. 'British Bulldog, can I have an autograph for my kid?' But I want to go home and I don't want to be the British Bulldog. I'm no star, not to me, I'm just the guy who got the job to be a professional wrestler.

At home I just want to be David Smith. When I go to pubs at home I'm normally okay, but it's when I go to these little towns that maybe people want to pick fights. They think, 'What have I got to lose? If I get beaten by the British Bulldog, maybe I can sue him.'

I got charged with assault up in Canada . . .

Diana Hart: It's not great at all. We keep hearing things about that guy, just carrying on the way he was that night . . .

Davey Boy Smith: My trial's in Calgary in January 1996.

Simon Garfield: He was accused of attacking a man called Kody Light in a drunken nightclub brawl. It was said that Light suffered brain injuries from the incident, and spent over a month in hospital. If convicted of aggravated assault Davey Boy Smith faced up to fourteen years in jail, but he was confident he wouldn't even get a fine.

Diana Hart: Davey is pretty remarkable. The way he wrestles, the work he does with kids.

Davey Boy Smith: I talk to dying kids. When I was in Britain in 1994, some kid was dying, he like died twice and they brought him back. All he wanted was a picture of me. They asked my mum, and she said, 'Well, he gets in tonight. He flies in from the States.'

So I drove in near Bradford somewhere, and I go see him, and he's dying of cancer, twelve years old. He knows he's dying too, because he says, 'I may die tomorrow, but I'm going to a place I'm going to be peaceful for the rest of my life.' I get all emotional and go, 'Jesus.' His mum and dad are there, and they start crying, and the kid goes, 'I want no one crying in this room. You're not going to cry, Bulldog!'

I'm sat there talking to him for three hours. Two days later he died. People don't see that side of what we do. He had British Bulldog wallpaper, bed sheets, shoes. I couldn't believe he had so much stuff on me. Everything was just me.

15

'Walked into that one,' said Robbie Brookside

Robbie Brookside: 'It's a serious thing, a life'

Simon Garfield: At Brent Town Hall, Wembley, in the large Oasis Room, a venue that would welcome the Chippendales the following day, I watched two wrestlers rehearse.

In the ring, in the centre of an empty hall, was Dave 'Fit' Finlay, a champion from Belfast, and a young Japanese trainee. Later in the evening, as Finlay bounced off the ropes into a powerslam, the MC would say, ' . . . and that's how Finlay got his nickname – he's just so fit!', but in training he seemed to be tired, all lager and pies, and he really had to push himself to get the legs working.

He showed the young Japanese lad a few tricks, how to cross-press with maximum weight, how to twist out from a headlock. Some of the time Finlay would do this in slow motion, so that the youngster could better follow the move. The choreography was most visible during the dropkicks, when contact was seldom made at all, despite the dramatic and anguished reaction on the face of the fall guy. If contact was made it was usually gentle, and against a puffed chest rather than a face. At the moment of contact one of the fighters would clap his hands or stamp a foot. I remember thinking that this was a far more skilful activity than simply engaging in a brawl.

It was about 7 pm. When the show began an hour later, there were only 120 people in, an appalling spectacle. The tickets were £6 each, the same price as three years ago. Any more and there would have been even fewer. It was the start of 1995 in England, an All Star Promotion run by Brian Dixon. This was practically all that was left. I remember looking around and feeling sad.

I followed Finlay and his apprentice backstage, and met Robbie Brookside, twenty-eight years old, very long light brown hair, quite good looking, with very intense eyes. By way of introduction, Brookside told me he had more or less split from his regular tag partner Doc Dean, and tonight would be paired with Stevie Jay. He was a little anxious, fearing a lack of communication could lose them the bout.

Then a stout Japanese man walked by in green trunks and cape. This was Japan's Mean Machine, over for a few weeks from Tokyo on a tour not only of Wembley, but of Croydon, Norwich, Mansfield and Rawtenstall. He spoke little English.

'Who you fight?' Robbie Brookside asked him in soft scally.

'Power Ranger!' said Japan's Mean Machine.

'Power Ranger?' Brookside repeated. 'He very good – a favourite.'

'Ah, I lose,' said Japan's Mean Machine, strangely happy at the prospect.

At 7.55 the lights dimmed in the auditorium. It was a dedicated crowd – several Bangladeshi families on a half-term treat, some retired couples, some middle-aged men who arrived on their own but knew each other and sat together, and about twenty children barely old enough to walk. There was some applause when the lights went down. A few whistled, and one man shouted, 'Oh no!'

There was over-amplified music. A tape went, 'Get ready to rumble! Music! Action!', followed by the tinny patriotic drill that accompanied Pathe newsreels, then a rap beat, then a song almost certainly called 'Let's Get Ready to Rum-Rum-Rumble' that went on for a very long time. A spotlight beamed around the audience, as a man in the balcony tried valiantly to transform the atmosphere from that of a memorial service to that of ITV's *Gladiators*, the programme often cited as televised wrestling's natural successor.

A person in a double-breasted suit and red-framed glasses climbed into the ring, told everyone his name, told us we were in for a great night and shouted, 'Match number one, and here come the wrestlers!' All heads turn to some plush red curtains at one end of the room. No wrestlers. Someone shouted, 'Mmmm, curtains!'

The MC said, 'a-a-a-nd play the first wrestler's music please!' Then there was another delay. The audience listened keenly. At the back of the hall came the sound of someone turning over a cassette. Then 'Blam-ba-la!! Blam-ba-la!!', the opening bars of 'Mr Vain', and the curtains parted to reveal Dale the Model Preston.

Preston was blond, tall and very pumped. He was wearing reflective shades and a black bow tie, and he had just oiled his chest. He walked to the ring very slowly, and glared and pouted at a member of the audience as he smoothed back his hair. One or two people in the audience pointed at him and laughed. One or two booed, and one or two cheered. Once in the ring, he handed his tie and shades to an elderly man in his corner in a red

shirt and very tight white trousers, acting as his 'second'.

'And the second wrestler's music, please!' Click. Another rap song, about working your body. An Indian man called Tiger Kashmir Singh appeared in a swish of curtain. Apart from his nationality, he sported no gimmicks. The fight commenced and, as might be expected, Dale the Model Preston had a gag linked to his nickname: he was vain and self-adoring, and the joke was that whenever Tiger Kashmir Singh made any contact with Dale the Model Preston's hair, the Model recoiled in horror, and asked someone in the audience for a mirror, and then spat on his palms to pat down his locks. I think he'd been watching Adrian Street tapes. This was a one-gag bout – Kashmir Singh never played the Bamboozled Indian card, or indeed the Tiger card – and so the laughter wore a little thin after the Model's hair had been ruffled several times.

The Model won through with one pinfall after about fifteen minutes. It was a fairly tedious match, and few in the crowd seemed to care much about the outcome. It seemed to say something about the state of the modern game that even during the first bout the good citizens of Wembley – starved, we were told, of wrestling in these parts for many months – found themselves looking at the wood panelling. Even with the hair gag, this was not really a contest with a story. The high point came when one man in the crowd yelled out, 'Fuck off back to Lincolnshire, Model!'

I noticed wrestling fans prided themselves on this sort of thing, a form of bespoke abuse seldom found in other entertainments, apart from boxing. As with boxing, place of birth is seen as somehow significant. Fans like to root for someone from their home town or county, but not half as much as they like to hurl crap at people who come from anywhere else. You can use all the stereotypes this way – mean Scots, bruising Irish, simple Cornishmen, gritty northerners, poofy southerners. As with most sports, anyone

hailing from Leicester seems to get a particularly bad deal. This happens in football, as fans chant (to the tune of 'Land of Hope and Glory'), 'We all follow the Chelsea, over land and sea – and Leicester!'

And it happens in wrestling. Dave 'Slappy' Shuds hailed from Leicester, and crowds would never let him forget it.

Obviously, it's not hard to guess a wrestler's calling card just from his nickname. As before, Dave Finlay's trademark is that he's fit, Jim 'Cry Baby' Breaks tantrums a lot, Brian 'Goldbelt' Maxine has a gold belt, Dave Shuds slaps people. The Power 'Restlin' Ranger's schtick is that he wrestles, or rather restles. This addition of a middle name may also be a lame attempt to avoid legal prosecution, although every judge in the world would have no doubt whatsoever that what we had next in the Oasis Room was copyright infringement of the highest order.

Power 'Restlin' Ranger came into the ring in full red bodystocking and a mask resembling a crash helmet. The Power Rangers were that season's kids' favourites, and every Saturday morning on television they kicked and karated all the rubber bad things the Japanese/American co-creators could throw at them. They always emerged victorious after twenty-five minutes packed with adventure, twenty-five minutes in which the Rangers did almost everything physically possible, except wrestling. The Power 'Restlin' Ranger came on to the incessant TV theme tune – 'Go Go Power Rangers, Go Go Power Rangers' – and it was clear that he would also win everything on offer.

Unlike the TV Rangers, who are teenaged and thin and hungry, the 'Restlin' Ranger moved as though he was at least forty-five, and had enjoyed way too many starch suppers. I suspected he was probably a rather bitter old wrestler who had never proved much of a draw when using his real name, a man who would not be missed if he was never seen in the ring again. In other words, it was not Kendo Nagasaki. There was no way he could keep going against Japan's Mean Machine for twenty-five minutes, so Japan's Mean Machine rolled over and died for him after ten.

Throughout the match Japan's Mean Machine had employed Japanese war cries, and whenever he got the 'Restlin' Ranger in any form of hold he would find the English for 'ASK HIM!', shorthand for 'Ask him if wishes to submit', or possibly 'Ask him if he's from Leicester.' The referee did ask him, and inevitably he said no, but when the tables were turned and it was the Ranger's turn to shout 'ASK HIM!', Japan's Mean Machine said 'YES!' and crumpled like origami at his feet. The young children were happy, and exclaimed 'Go Go Power Ranger!' as their hero hobbled back behind the drapes. A man in the crowd shouted, 'Fuck you, Ranger!'

Then Robbie Brookside and Stevie Jay bounced on, to fight the Notorious Superflys, two unshaven, burly, uncouth, ugly men from the Norwich area. This was a riotous contest. Though Brookside and Jay were about to lose (Brookside was carrying a shoulder injury from an awkward fall the week before), it was clear that this was the bout of the evening, a perfect match of storyline and action. Brookside was the closest the wrestling game had to a genuine hero for the teens. The Power Ranger appealed to the six-year-olds, but the thirteen- and fourteen-year-olds who crushed up against their pop stars in their bedrooms at night would surely get moist for Robbie Brookside, if only they knew about him. I had heard he had a huge following in Liverpool, and fans would really scream at him, but elsewhere he was mostly just another bit of half-decent dynamism. He already had the flowing hair and good physique and keen attitude. What he needed was great marketing, and a feverish manager.

At Brent Town Hall he fell victim to weak communication with his new partner, and to two dirty opponents who would do everything illegal when the referee's back was turned. Brookside was not happy when he left the ring.

Dave Finlay then beat Dave Rocky Taylor, who sportingly grabbed the microphone at the end of the contest to acknowledge the level of the victor's extraordinary fitness.

And so the scene was set for the ten-man King of the Ring Rumble, a steal from America. There were no falls, no submissions, no time limit, not even a referee. This was because there was no room for a referee: the ten wrestlers I had just seen all piled into the ring together and started fighting in a free-for-all.

When people went over the rope they did it with so much relief and verve and self-propulsion that they fooled no one. But the kids seemed to love it, not least because it looked like a Wild West barroom brawl, and provided the chance for the settling of old scores. So Tiger Kashmir Singh could work on weakening the strapped knee of Dale the Model Preston, and Brookside and Jay took much delight in hurling out the Notorious Superflys. And they liked it because the Power 'Restlin' Ranger survived to face Dave 'Fit' Finlay in the final showdown. As a collective, the audience had one question on its mind: would Finlay be fit enough? It turned out that he was so fit, he was fit up. The Power 'Restlin' Ranger won because he had to win: Brian Dixon clearly saw the children as his future customers, and even future fathers in years to come, and there was no way he was going to send them home tearful. You can

Brookside hits a man with funny shoes: 'I don't want to kill anyone, because I've got to face them after'

quote all you like about 'leave them wanting more', but if the hero loses on a low-profile night like tonight, that's the end, and it will be on the 0898 Wrestlecall hotline before you know it, and try selling your 'Restlin' merchandise then. For fitness is no match against fate – ask anyone: in wrestling, some things were just meant to be.

Robbie Brookside: The crowd was rubbish that night. The bad crowd, and my shoulder . . . I just couldn't be fucked. But if I don't fight, I don't eat. I've got no insurance and no savings. You'll never believe how little money I get.

Things will be different at St George's in Liverpool next month. I'm back with the Doc, the old team. The crowd go crazy up there. My mum will come, though my dad's dead now. And I miss him, though he hated the wrestling at first.

My dad was a footballer, he played four games for Preston. From the age of three months I was kicking footballs. When I was eight I was playing against fifteen-year-old guys. When I was ten I got into school teams and then I got a trial for Liverpool Schools. I played with them for about three years. Everything revolved around football. It was my dad's ambition.

But I was an Everton fan, and I used to watch them whenever I could. I collected programmes, and had every single Everton home programme for fifteen years, all the binders. I had every England Wembley programme for twenty years.

When I wasn't watching or playing football on a Saturday I used to watch *World of Sport* with Dickie Davies with the grey streaks. I was always intrigued by the wrestling. Unfortunately my dad used to come in from work just after four and he used to say, 'Get that shite off!' He used to put it over to the rugby, and he hardly ever let me watch it. Whenever he went out the room it was back on the wrestling, but then when he came back, click again. I was about ten. We never had a portable.

My auntie used to go to a place called the Liverpool Stadium. It was like a Laurel and Hardy building, built in the 1880s, a real fighting venue that staged championship boxing – John Conteh won his title there, an 8,000–10,000 seater. My auntie used to watch weekly shows there, put on by none other than Brian Dixon. In about 1979 I pleaded with my mum to let Auntie Vera take me along, and I got my pocket money and she said okay.

It was in the city centre, the old part by the old docks. A long street, and you walked up to it and you could see 'The Stadium' in big letters, and for a boy of fourteen like me it was the most exciting thing in my life.

I went inside and it blew me away. There was a knockout tournament for a middleweight championship. A fellow called John Cortez, a very good grafter, won. Adrian Street was there, Jackie Pallo, but we won't give any messages to Jackie Pallo other than, 'Die, you old bastard.'

I just fell in love with the whole thing. I was never really a 'he punched him, referee' kind of fan, but I liked to watch the way the wrestlers could control the crowd, and the different moods they had, the different personalities. The next week I went back, and the week after I went again.

Brookside with his partner Doc Dean: 'Life is hard, Life is pain'

My training sessions for Liverpool Schools unfortunately fell on the same day, so within a month I never went training once. They sent a letter to my school and my parents, saying if I didn't turn up they'd kick me out. And I didn't turn up. It was the worst thing that could have ever happened to my dad. He hated wrestling at the best of times. I was so pressurized to stop going.

My dad got talking to some of my mates and said, 'Look, he's wasting his life here, he's got the chance of making something of himself with football. So go put the knockers in, go and do a spoiler.' So my mates came to a show with me, and they went up to a wrestler and pointed at me and said, 'That kid down there thinks it's not real.' He said, 'If he thinks it's not real get him to Kirby Stadium on Sunday.' Kirby's an overspill area.

When I went in there were about ten lads, and a big mat in the centre, but no ropes. Every schoolboy can tell you what it's like to have a punch in the face or a kick, but that wrestler just got me in front of everyone, and I felt like a piece of turkey. He had me in knots, basically just humiliated me. I think my father just wanted to put me off wrestling; I don't think he wanted me to get beat up. Three minutes felt like two hours. I was blowing, I was spitting blood, and afterwards I couldn't move my jaw. I remember the pain the next day at school and not being able to eat the cake.

But I thought I'd go back next week. The same thing happened again – they done me in. And on the third week they done me in. On the fourth week they said, 'We'll start showing you a few things.' So they showed me how to put the holds on. But they were really into amateur wrestling, and I told them I wasn't really into that.

I then went to a gym in Rhyl, North Wales, the last summer vacation before I left school. You learn the basic things, like how to link up properly. It looks so easy when you see it, but you get in the ring and your head just goes 'What?' You have no idea what to do, or what to do next. So I learnt how to take an arm. Early on I kept on thinking, What the hell have I done, taking this up? The people I had played with in Liverpool Schools were beginning to make a living – like Ian Bishop playing for West Ham, Johnny Morrissey went to Tranmere, we played London when Tony Adams was there. They're making a buck or five now.

My dad gave me no support whatsoever, and he made it clear how disappointed he was. We still got on, but as soon as we mentioned football or wrestling it got a bit nasty. He was working at the post office. Preston had offered him terms, but in the fifties football wasn't the lucrative job it is today. He wanted to see the world, so he joined the army and went out to Korea. So basically he did what I did – pushed football to one side.

I went to see Brian Dixon and he didn't want to know. He kept coming out with excuses. The only guy who would give me a chance was a fellow called Bobby Barron, and he ran a fairground booth on Blackpool Pleasure Beach. You had to take people on from the crowd – the old style. If you got beat it's your money gone. If the punters survive three three-minute rounds they get £50, and that comes out of your wages too.

They can kick and punch and head-butt, and so you have to keep them at arms length and get them on the floor. You have to get your arms and legs inside them and start stretching them. There was a Scottish guy, and this was very scary. At the front of the Pleasure Beach there's the Horseshoe Showbar, and we were always upstairs. But for some reason one day there was another show booked, and so we had to go downstairs to this Diamond Lil's bar. At the bar this day there were about fifteen drunken Glasgow chaps bawling away.

I used to wear a mask at this time. If they saw my face . . . I was quite tall but I would have looked so young. I was known as the Masked Marauder.

I was doing all right that night, I had just slapped a submission on this one guy, and then one of the Glasgow lads is pushed forward by the others, and you can see he doesn't really want to fight, but they're all goading him on. So he says he'll do it. The MC asks him, 'Have you been drinking?' and he said, 'A couple.' So he gets in, and throws a couple of punches. I leg-dived him, got him on the floor, got round the back of him and wrenched his head back as hard as I could. He was in so much pain he actually pissed himself. So I've won the match, and the next thing I know two of his mates have jumped the ring and jumped on my back. They had my mask off. Then they're all in the ring, and the security people get in, and it's a huge bloody fight. There were beer glasses flying all over. Got out of it just about.

I went back to my lodgings and I was in such pain I couldn't sleep. I'd slammed the base of my back, and when I got up my whole spine was raw. I walked around and thought I'd try some Ralgex on it and I screamed. I thought I was going to die. It was the first of a thousand real pains.

Then Brian came up one day and said, 'All right, I'm going to give you a chance.'

Brian Dixon: You would never meet anyone more enthusiastic about wrestling than I've been. I've promoted for about twenty-five years. I must have promoted at almost every public hall in Britain, with the exception of places of worship.

But there is no road out of it now, it's the lowest ebb. Anything I say about wrestling will not be positive. I'm thinking of stopping altogether between October and December when we may only get a hundred customers a night. April is bad too. I daren't raise the prices. January to March and May to September are still just about okay, and in the summer we do the Butlins holiday camps, but the big names won't touch Butlins now.

I've never been in a situation before where I've had shows booked all over the country and haven't been able to find the wrestlers to attract the crowds. I book the venues twelve months in advance, and have to cancel them without the public ever knowing.

Without television we're kidding ourselves that it's got a chance for much longer. We've just survived on the likes of Nagasaki and Haystacks, who were TV names that people remember, but Kendo's retired and the others are getting older and older and I feel they're yesterday's news.

Now we have the Power Ranger. The Power Ranger was my idea. I can take the credit for it and I think it's a tremendous thing. You do have to jump on the bandwagon. The first time I realized we really had something was when the Power Ranger walked into a hall two months ago and the crowd went absolutely mad. He was mobbed by kids. Now, I've promoted every wrestler in the British Isles of superstar status, and I've never seen anything like this. I thought, We could really do something with this fellow, this fellow could really go to town.

The fellow who's done the Power Ranger until now walked out as himself at Bristol last night and . . . absolute silence. I'm looking for someone even more flamboyant to do him now, and soon there will be not only a red Ranger, but a blue Ranger.

Wrestlers must communicate. If you haven't got eye contact with the crowd . . . Brookside and Doc Dean take the piss out of me for this: eye contact – you have to ask the audience all the time what you should do. The wrestler has got to involve the person on the front row. It's the only way they'll remember you.

The best friend I ever had was Mark Rocco. There are so few solid people in this game, and Rocco was always so loyal. He'd go to the other end of the world to fulfil my needs. He's a hell of a loss. If you went in the ring with him he'd make you look like a million dollars, and then he'd kill you. What he did was sensational – wrestlers would come out and watch him, the ultimate compliment, because wrestlers never gave compliments to anyone. He was ten years too soon in this job.

He's retired now, a successful businessman in Tenerife. He almost died in the ring. He was wrestling at Worthing, and he looked terrible when he turned up. All green. He was told not to go on, but he wouldn't listen. His heart gave out. He did actually die, but they brought him back. He was told he would never wrestle again, and he was devastated.

I thought it was all up for me too. I suppose Brookside is the closest we've got to Rocco now, in terms of the physical attributes. I'm terribly proud of Brookside, what he's achieved, though I always tell him he lacks the self-discipline.

Robbie Brookside: My first two years for Brian were hell. It was still on television, and from the scraps at Blackpool I was suddenly elevated to big bills in London and Liverpool and Manchester. I fought Rollerball Rocco, Mighty John Quinn, Tony St Clair, Johnny Saint. At that time I was six foot two and about twelve or thirteen stone, so good height, but also quite lean. One night I'd be on with a heavyweight and the next with a lightweight. Brian knew this new soap was starting, so he called me Brookside for the image. On my cheques it's still Brooks. I'm always asked on local radio by those prat DJs, 'Why's your name Robbie Brookside?' And I go, 'Because it is,' followed by silence.

Making friends was very hard, wrestlers can be so cold and excluding. It would have been lovely just to have had a normal apprenticeship, just to have had to make tea and go to look for tartan paint, but it doesn't happen like that in the wrestling job. I'd be sixteen or seventeen, on the road for a week just travelling the motorways, and you'd wake up and have frying oil in your mouth, and they'd burn you and nick all your gear. I think it was a test to show how much you wanted a life like that.

They were always putting Ex-Lax in my tea – a favourite. I had to carry all the bags and I was the sponsored wrestler. In those days there was some sponsorship, and Brian's people were sponsored by Ben Truman, and I had to dress up as Ben Truman with a Dick Turpin hat and a dressing gown with Ben Truman 1666 on it, and I had to wear this as I went into the ring. Before the fight I had to give all these badges out to the kids. Plus I had to carry round all the stuff to build the ring, the spanners and other bits of metal. The main instigator was Brian. In the end I had to get away, got a job for the summer at the Liverpool garden festival. It was nice: good money and they treated me as a human being.

The holiday camps were very bad. One time they just got me on the floor by the dressing rooms at Minehead, took everything off me apart from my shorts, and tied me up with this washing line. There was a wrestler called the Convict who had handcuffs and shackles, and they used those and also gagged me. They went on Radio Butlin and said, 'We've got a missing wrestler – can you keep an eye out for him.' Hours later an old lady found me and shouted and within two minutes there were four hundred kids around me, all pointing.

I quit several times. In those days there were real stars in the ring, people made famous by television, and they wanted you to prove yourself to them. I should have just turned round and smacked the first guy who was trying it on with me, but I thought I was doing the right thing. I gave them a lot of respect, and I shouldn't have done that.

As far as the business goes, there is no money left in the kitty. We don't even talk about wage rises now. When I was younger I was on about £50 a week – could be one match for that, could be six. Nowadays I get paid per fight and some weeks I don't earn at all. I'd be too embarrassed to tell you how much I got.

My friend Steve Regal is out in the States at the moment, and he says that when the British guys go out there they get so much respect, because they can wrestle. They know how to put a hold on. They're not just dick dancers turned wrestlers. When Regal went to America he said I should come with him a few years back, but I said, 'I'm never going, we've got the best wrestling country in the world here,' and I really did believe we could make something of it. And up to a point I still do. The future is in making the bouts harder, more aggressive, more technical. Bollocks to all that American crap. The twenty-five-year-olds would come back if we did that.

It bugs me now that I know we could turn this thing around if we had the right people behind us. I was watching waterskiing on television, and the sponsorship deals that they get . . . In wrestling there's corner bags, a ring, the apron, and they could all have some company's name on them.

In Japan and Mexico it's so well organized. So much more professional. Keep the mystique. But in England there is no mystique now – wrestlers go out into the hall after they've been on, or before, and sit down with a cup of tea. But they shouldn't really mix like that. There's no discipline, so slack. There are too many cowboys, too many fat old geriatrics in the ring who should have died five years ago. When people see that they say, 'Well if this is British wrestling I never want to see it again.'

Simon Garfield: Brookside was the finest ambassador British wrestling could hope for, and seldom missed an opportunity to talk up his profession. He gave interviews to local papers and local radio wherever he went, pleading for a bit of investment to revive his devastated world. Listening to him, and watching him fight, it was possible to believe that wrestling still had a future.

Robbie Brookside: It's the people who don't give their all who give us a bad name. Every sport has people like that, tossers, but it gets blown out of proportion in our sport. If someone doesn't want to hurt me, no problem, but I'm going to go out and beat them. I'm not going to go out and break their legs – I don't want to hurt anyone to that extent. I don't want to kill anyone, because I've got to face them after, out of the ring. When you're in the ring no problem, but when you've cooled down, and they go home to the wife and kids and they work as a postman or whatever, then I feel a bit cruel.

Here's the tape I was telling you about, a match in Wales. I'm in against Lee Thomas, a local man. That's Brian Dixon refereeing, or

Brian George as he calls himself. Not bad at it.

So here we go, and straight away we're going for the holds, so you can tell it's going to be clean and technical, no mucking about. That's always a favourite to put on first, a headlock, a good old-fashioned move, you can do so many things with it. He picks me up again now . . . shoots me off . . . I could have dropped an elbow there but I know he's going to get up, so I build up speed and hit him with a body check. Straight away I know that I'm taller than him so that if I come off the ropes and hit him he's going to go down. I'm confident at this stage . . . whup! . . . that's just to let him know that I'm there. You meet people who can't relate to that move there, I'm putting pressure on his shoulder, I've just twisted his arm out, that's just a little feeler. I've gone from the arm there to the neck, pressing down on his head and trying to keep his back straight . . . pulling back on his head now. If most people had these moves done to them they could relate to what's going on, relate to the pain. That's a full nelson, always effective if you put it on properly, right in the middle at the back of his head.

I'm not even eating his lunch yet. I'm keeping on him, that's all I'm doing. I want a small package and a pinfall, but I haven't got the leg yet. If I went in and won it in the first few minutes I'd be undermining myself really. Ooooh, I get one back for my troubles, but it's only on the chest. I'm dictating the pace all the time, eating his lunch now. Side suplex on his head!! He's gone there, totally gone, you see the legs aren't kicking. He's a nice lad, and now he probably realizes the error of his ways, but he's too keen, thinks he can do me, and he needed to have a bit of a lesson. There's this other good lad coming through called James Mason, and he's a really great prospect, only fifteen, and I'm absolutely buzzing with hope for him, but there are so few.

This guy here . . . your performance depends on your opponent. I can raise my performance ten-fold going on with Finlay. He can go from first to fifth gear without even thinking. If you're on with Finlay it's very hard, because he's always dictating the pace on account of his fitness. But this guy . . . I was fighting Finlay in Worthing last week, and doing moves that I couldn't believe. I thought, Nah, this is far too good for Worthing. But you just did them, because you think bollocks, this guy is hurting me. And Finlay does hurt you. With Finlay you're always going to get hurt. The way I hurt my shoulder is that he shoulder-drived me onto the canvas. He got me in a piledrive, and drove me down at an angle. The physiotherapy has already cost £85. And last night he gave me this gash.

That's a sleeper, no that's not a sleeper . . . he's starting to get out of it there. Watch what he does now. He should throw me for a Boston or something, but he's working my neck – that's no good. He should be coming for my back, I want him to come for my back . . . if it's a one-sided match it's terrible.

I've faced the Doc in a ladder match at the Fairfield Halls. They suspend £500 from the ring light in a bag, and they put a ladder at the back of the hall. So you have to nail your opponent, get out of the ring, get the ladder, put it up in the ring, and get the money. All while your opponent is out or down. So I got the Doc out, grabbed the ladder. But of course as soon as I got the ladder in the ring, he comes off the top rope. I grabbed the money, he kicked the ladder, I dropped the money outside the ring and he just fell on it. The crowd erupted.

There's a double one there, I'm bending him back . . . people submit from that very regular. I'm not putting that much pressure on – you can break someone's back doing that. I don't really want to get a submission out of that, not right for the rhythm of the match.

He's tired now, feeling it, so straight away I'm on his back. That's the mark of a good wrestler – he knows when to punish. On his head, on his head, figure four, but I've got it on loose and just let go. Now he has pain on the back of his leg, and neck and back and arms. Timing's the essence, you can take someone too quick. That's it really, the back of his head – the pain he's going through there . . . I don't think he wrestled again after this. Walked into that one. Right, the end is nigh. Whooosh, woof, I'm twisting it, that's it, there, off the ropes, there! A very satisfying bout. I did what I set out to do.

Simon Garfield: It was dinner time in the Brooks household, a midterrace off the Scotland Road. St George's Hall would be opening its doors in forty-five minutes. Brookside's mother brought in large plates of chilli and rice. From the kitchen Robbie fetched a huge tub of bodybuilding supplements – dried egg mixed with nutrients and twenty other things. He read the ingredients in disbelief as he whisked in milk. Possibly for my benefit, his mother chided him for not becoming a footballer and earning decent money. Brookside showed me pictures of his late father, and then I got a proud tour of his record collection, heavy in punk and thrash metal. Many of the bands had the words Death or Destroy or some form of Armageddon in their name.

After our meal, he scuttled around under the stairs assembling his kit, throwing crumpled Lurex into a holdall. He said that he's having a new kit made, and was sorry it wasn't ready for tonight. There was a red mask in his bag. 'I tell you,' he said with horror, 'I was the Power Ranger last week.'

I drove him to the venue, and on the way he said, 'For all the effort I've put into wrestling, what I've had back is very minimal, especially in this country. I try to put on a good show, but at times I admit I just think, Bollocks – I'll take a finish here. I just want to make something of myself . . . before some doctor turns round and says that's it for me. I'm knackered now. Every joint in my body aches. My physio says I've got the body of a fifty-year-old. I've got maybe ten years left, ten good years. This wrestling isn't a joke for me, it's a serious thing, a life.'

When it was completed in 1855, Queen Victoria called St George's Hall 'worthy of ancient Athens'. At its heart lies the Great Hall, the largest public reception space in Britain. The sunken encaustic floor contained thirty thousand tiles; the ten chandeliers are said to be the largest ever made. There were about nine hundred people in, as many children as adults. Many had come specifically to see Robbie Brookside reunited with his old friend and tag partner Ian Doc Dean.

There was a small groan as the MC announced that the Imposing Undertaker would not be appearing as scheduled, something about his back. His replacement was billed as a regular crowd pleaser, an ever-popular attraction, but turned out to be a fat middle-aged man no one appeared to have ever heard of.

His opponent was Mysterious King Kendo, and the mystery was how anyone could rip off Kendo Nagasaki so thoroughly, and so incompetently. Mysterious King Kendo wore similar clothes to Nagasaki – mask, cape, leggings – and he came into the ring with a sword, just like his mentor. There was no salt throwing, a Nagasaki trademark, and he only had a fraction of Nagasaki's power or presence. Beneath Mysterious King Kendo's mask lay only a sham of a wrestler, someone who wasn't enjoying his fighting at all. Who was he really? No one cared. He beat the middle-aged unknown, but no one cared much about that either.

On a normal night, a night without Brookside and Dean's tag-team challenge, the next match would have been top of the bill: Red Power Ranger versus Dave 'Fit' Finlay. And on a normal night when Finlay wrestles, Finlay wins. But the Power Ranger was again welcomed with such tiny screams of delight, and much genuine handslapping and hem-touching, and had already proved himself unbeatable on the merchandise stall earlier in the evening, that fate intervened once more and ensured that Finlay left the hall shouting about revenge.

Next up was James Mason, the great fifteen-year-old hope billed as the 'east London heartbreaker'. Mason ran towards the ring in a sparkling rainbow leotard, slapping young hands as he threw himself over the ropes. It was unlikely that many people here had seen him before, or even heard of him, but he came on like the biggest star in the world. I think Brian Dixon had told him that the way to be remembered was to make eye contact with the crowd, and touch them if he could. It didn't look as though the people really wanted to touch him, but he had blond hair, a broad smile, blue eyes and he demanded to be adored. He was the keenest human I had ever seen. I feared for him.

He was fighting the British Bushwhacker. I had seen the New Zealand Bushwhackers fight on American television, and this man in Liverpool was a very pale imitation. He was much smaller, much skinnier, older, and he drew his humour not so much from primitive rural life (as did the originals) but from *Carry On*. He pretended he was more stupid than he was, and behaved as if this was his first fight, and he didn't quite understand the rules. He kept on falling over and hitting the referee. He found strange things in his trousers, including a rubber chicken. The one thing he had copied from the New Zealanders was their walk, a big-striding gait with crooked, furious arms going up-down like a steam piston. It was no contest. Mason couldn't understand this guy, and so didn't watch his back enough, and got caught out on an easy pinfall. He then bounced off, as happy as he had come in, another few quid in his pocket, a lift sorted back to his mother's flat in Wapping, his hopes perfectly intact. He still couldn't believe his luck: fresh from school, and already a professional wrestler.

Frank Casey: I'm forty-five and I've been in the business fifteen years. I wasn't an athlete by any means. I always liked acting. I had a few gimmicks, the Fugitive, the Convict, the arrows on the pyjamas and the handcuffs. I've been a Ghostbuster. But when I saw the Bushwhackers they took over my life. I've never seen them live, but on TV they were doing something unorthodox. So I got the gear, and when I put the Bushwhacker stuff on I was transformed.

Brian Dixon will tell you that I've got 2 per cent wrestling ability, but 98 per cent entertainment ability. That's what matters to me. I do worry about it before I go on, whether I can get the crowd up, because that's my part, why he puts me in the ring. In the old days I used to have to do six rounds of wrestling, pure wrestling – not for me.

When Brian first saw me do the Bushwhacker he said, 'That's a good little gimmick, that will maybe last six months.' That was five, six years ago. The clothes were just basic army gear, easy to get in Liverpool. I saw a picture of them in a magazine carrying a big French loaf of bread, so I thought I'd have something like that as well, so I bought the rubber chicken. That nearly got robbed in St George's Hall.

I thought I was going to have copyright problems, but nothing. I wanted to get hold of the Bushwhackers' music, and you can get all of the WWF entrance songs on one tape. But as I don't have credit cards or anything I asked my sister Pauline to phone America and order it for me. When I called to check she'd done it she said, 'Not only that, but I also told the WWF that you were going to be the Bushwhacker over here.' I thought that would kill it stone dead, but the tape came through, and I use it, and I've heard nothing more. I love that music. Once I hear that, the character takes over and the arms start going.

The work commitment now doesn't allow me to do as much as

I'd like to, the bedroom fitting. But Brian's so quiet now anyway, and he has to look after the full-time men first. It makes me feel very sad what's happened. Straightforward wrestling always used to bore me, but now even the characters have gone. The lads have been down for years, and they're drifting away. Even for me . . . there are hardly any people left that make me want to watch them like I used to.

Simon Garfield: Brookside's and Dean's entrance was greeted by chants of 'Liverpool! Liverpool!', and no one was more vocal than Brookside himself. The Superflys were jeered as they paraded their championship belts above their heads, and people in the audience shouted things like, 'Kiss 'em goodbye, stupid.' Brookside reckoned this was the sixtieth time they had met.

It was a hard fight, with much top-rope action and flying mares and clotheslines. It was the best of three falls, and the bout upped in emotion when the Superflys got the first, and the Liverpool Lads the last two. They came back somehow, to great cheers.

I talked to Brookside's mother as the crowd thinned. She had been drinking throughout the evening and was now in fine form, kissing everyone, repeating her observation that her granddaughter looked like Marilyn Monroe whenever her skirt puffed up with the air from the heating grilles around the hall. Mitzi Mueller approached her in a tight green suit to say hello. Mrs Brooks said her son was a tag-team champion again.

I congratulated Brookside when he reappeared with his new belt. He seemed surprised that I had entertained any doubts. He didn't seem to be a much happier person than the one I'd driven to the hall three hours before. It wasn't like boxing, where the new champion held his arms high, and held interviews, and hugged his opponent and talked of a big purse to come. The result of his victory would not appear in any of the Sunday papers. Next week he'd be fighting somewhere else, for smaller money. And there would be fewer people watching.

*

Four months later I travelled with Robbie Brookside, Doc Dean and Steve Prince to a wrestling bout in Germany. In fact, I drove them most of the way in my car, until I got exhausted and Prince took over. I'm still not quite sure what I was hoping to find, beyond further evidence of disintegration.

We set off at a ridiculous hour – 4.30 am – from Brookside's girl-friend's house in Sittingbourne, Kent. Brookside said this early hour was 'a bit punk rock'.

We were heading for Hostenbach, near Saarbrucken, near the border with Luxembourg, a tiny town celebrating the fiftieth anniversary of its football team. The celebrations lasted a long weekend, and the Monday night finale was a load of blokes from England taking on huge local Germans, not at football but in wrestling, or as they called it, catch.

On the Dover ferry the wrestlers had the farmhouse cook-up. Doc Dean had two pints of beer. When we landed in France they talked of how they used to fly over, and were met at the airport and had nice hotels. This was until Klondyke Jake came on the scene.

Robbie Brookside: Jake's from the Midlands, another hairy wrestler, same mould as Haystacks but not quite as big, with two wrestling sons, Jake Junior and David. When he first came over to fight for a German promoter he told him he could do it far more cheaply by coming in a van with three or four other wrestlers in the back. This was indeed so much cheaper, so end of all flights.

One of Klondyke Jake's sons wrestles as the Imposing Undertaker, but it's a very poor imitation of the American – smaller, lighter, doesn't even do the sit-up. Of course his dad always says, 'Can't bloody tell the difference – remarkable!'

Simon Garfield: The wrestlers said the German trips are still worth-while, even after Klondyke Jake. They earn four times as much as they do for Brian Dixon, about £120 when the mark is strong. This is the tenth trip they've made.

They talked about dodgy promoters they had known. Brookside told a story of a show in Derby, where the promoter tried to branch out from wrestling into pop music, and advertised Cliff Richard in a local theatre. Of course Cliff was never contracted, but his name drew a packed crowd, and when they grew restless the promoter put on a cassette of his greatest hits and left the hall.

There was chat about women throughout the journey. On the early morning road through France there were plenty they'd like to give one to, plenty they didn't fancy at all. One of them had brought girlie mags – '*Whitehouse* – that's a good one.' Doc Dean had received a letter from a girl he met at a holiday camp: 'Hello Babe, At this moment in time I'm sat on my bed with my quilt over my head and a torch as it's thundering like mad and I hate it. I think my shed is gonna fall down. You left your boxers in my bed.'

The wrestlers talked of Brian Dixon. They admired him, they resented the American merchandise he flogged from the ring between bouts, they criticized the lack of a business plan.

Steve Prince, who often wrestled as Soldier Boy in a tag team called Task Force One, said he'd be both Soldier Boy and the Egyptian Mummy tonight. He also said he had a Power Rangers costume in his bag.

Brookside frequently regretted forgetting his punk and speed tapes. He said he brought T-shirts with him to trade with the Germans, and held them up during a stop. One read 'Infest'. Another, 'Life is hard, Life is pain'.

Klondyke Jake: 'Can't bloody well tell the difference – remarkable'

When we arrived other British wrestlers were already stretching in the sun. Klondyke Jake had brought over his two sons, a referee, a fat man who called himself Donk the Clown, and Tiger Kashmir Singh. The paper flyers announced the local talent: Robby Ganseuer, Chris the Lightning Kid and Eddi Steinblock.

The ring was being set up in a marquee behind a football pitch. The promoter wondered which wrestler I was. Steve Prince said that he bet I always wanted to become a wrestler, to which I said, 'Of course.'

Frank Casey:
'Pure wrestling –
not for me'

Prince's real name was Pringle, and he worked for the council in Stoke-on-Trent counselling and rehousing gypsies. He was thirty-six, and he'd been wrestling for fifteen years. Of course it's bent, he said, but if you get it right it can be the best entertainment. His knees can get bad, and when his little daughter sees him hobbling around at home 'sometimes she brings me my tea'. He wrestled mostly for his three kids, to pay for their new shoes or toys, whatever they want.

Prince said he was very concerned about the future for Brookside and Dean. They have no other jobs. 'If I ever win the lottery I'll make sure that they're looked after, I'll buy them a motor each, as thanks for all the work they've done.'

The kids and parents loved the show. Donk the Clown entered with green hair and pinned the ref. The Egyptian Mummy appeared to dark operatic music and strangled a German with his bandages. The English Undertaker looked nothing like the original. Tiger

Singh travelled all this way and lasted two minutes. The Liverpool Lads beat Prince and another of Klondyke Jake's sons two falls to one.

On the way back, loaded with currency and small bottles of lager, the wrestlers discussed women and football and how they'd spend the dawning day. Brookside said, 'Didn't that bastard *Jackie Pallo* used to drive a Saab?'

James Mason: 'The crowd ain't there now that Daddy's gone'

16

'Wrestling is all there is for me now,' said James Mason

James Mason: I was born 22 June '79. I've always been from Bermondsey. I went to Walworth School down the Old Kent Road. I began going to shows when I was seven, and my favourite was always Big Daddy. Me and my dad travelled round the halls, as many as three or four shows a week, and when we got home we both felt we'd had a good night out. There used to be a different story each show. I've always liked to watch two people fighting, but not violently. I never went out Saturdays so I could watch it.

As we travelled round we got to know people, and we used to get there early and I began to help putting the rings up. I got friendly with one of the referees, and did the rings with him for about six months when I was thirteen, getting a bit of pocket money just to cover my food.

About half an hour before the doors opened [on the professional fights] I used to bump around a bit in the ring, and a few of the wrestlers would show me a few moves, and one night Brian was watching and he said he thought I was about ready for my first fight and that in a couple of weeks he'd put me on.

It was 29 July '93 at Worthing, the Pier Pavilion, on with Darren Walsh. I was fourteen. I looked terrible, a skimpy black leotard. The fear all that week before the fight was very bad. Not really about getting hurt, but about whether I'd remember what I'd learnt, how the crowd would react. I only did about eight or nine minutes and got pinned, just the nerves got to me. Everything a blur. I went to take his hand, and I missed his arm. My nose was bleeding from a nasty bump.

For my second fight, at a holiday camp, I faced the Warlord, about twenty stone, and was terrified again and lost. In my first year I only won about 2 per cent of the fights. But within the last six or seven months I've actually started to win a few more. About once every four months. With tags I do better – with Flash Barker, Darren Walsh and Julie Star. They do a lot of the work and sometimes I might get one fall.

I'm still on very low pay because I'm only fifteen. The pay's nothing to be proud of, in fact a bit degrading. But I can't tell you how much. Your wages are top secret in wrestling – I haven't even told my mum and dad. A lot of the time I travel by train and I get the child fares, and I get it back from the promoter after the fight. Always cash, sometimes in an envelope. It makes no difference how you do, if you win or lose. I'm not insured. I'm not earning sufficient to pay for it.

Wrestling is all there is for me now, and I want to do it for as long as I can. Other lads tell me that the only future is trying to go to Germany. Obviously if you can get to America you've got it made.

Simon Garfield: He lived with his mother in a small flat on a dark estate near Wapping. His father left some years ago, but they still see each other. His mother brought in some tea and set the video to record *Bottom* for James. She said she's frightened about him getting hurt, but she tries to be supportive. She attends as many local shows as she can.

James Mason: My real name is James Atkins. At my first bout the MC John Harris said it wasn't really a wrestling name. He came up with James Mason, a name that people would remember. But then I was wrestling for Oric Williams in Wales and he said James Mason was a boring actor and that people would think I was a boring wrestler. So I was called Jesse James out there. I like Mason myself, and by coincidence it's my mum's maiden name.

I haven't really got a gimmick apart from my babyface, and I think Brian wants to keep that image – the young innocent lad that everyone can love.

When people come up to me and say it's all fixed, which happens all the time, it's a real insult. When I got slammed by Klondyke Kate last week it was just terribly painful, and it jarred my back and I could really feel my ribs cave in and felt awful when I got up the next day. Of course we also have to give people something to think about when they go home, and make them want to come again for the rematch. Brian will tell us what to do sometimes, but it's not rehearsed like some people say. So it's an insult, especially when you've been working so hard in the ring to provide entertainment.

When I used to watch it on television I had my suspicions like everyone else, and you think it must be rigged. But when you actually get in there you find it's 99 per cent real, and you take some knocks. There is a bit of pain there if you take backdrops and body-slams. But I only look after my own matches – I don't know how other people organize theirs. The stock wrestler's response when people say it is all fake is to take them in the ring and give them a good hiding. The worst person to say that to would be Fit Finlay. He'd drag you into the ring and hurt you very much.

I've got maximum respect for Brookside. I've got a long way to go before I get as good as him. He'll get a trial in Mexico soon and I wish him all the luck. He's the best that Britain has to offer – so seasoned. I've had some pranks played on me, but not as much as Brookside. Once I fell asleep in Ireland, and I'd had a bit to drink, and I woke up to find my eyebrows shaved off. That annoyed me.

Once I wrestled for Dale Martin – Max Crabtree – at Croydon and there were less than a hundred in. He used to do three shows a night, but now he's lucky to be doing three a month. But any Max Crabtree shows I've gone to in the last few years, they're just dead, the crowd ain't there now that Daddy's gone.

There'll always be a market for wrestling, it will never die completely. Once I wrestled in front of eight people in a caravan park – can't get no worse than that.

Klondyke Kate: I feel sorry for young James, for the young guys coming in now. At least I saw some good years. Now I've got two more jobs and then I'm finishing. I won't do no more. The love of it's missing. I've been dancing in the fountains at Hastings at three in the morning. Now it's drive to a show, wrestle, drive back. The heart of it's gone.

I might go back to school. I've got no qualifications whatsoever. I'm very interested in people. I'm very interested in psychology. I think I'm a good listener. I've been an agony aunt to a lot of wrestlers. I've always wanted to write a book about wrestling, but I can't word it. What I'd really like to get into is acting, another dodgy lifestyle. I've done one film with Margi Clarke, *Blonde Fist*, the prison bully, a speaking part.

Someone said to me, 'Why don't you come and work on my market stall?' I'm not doing that. Is that what it's come to? A market stall? I'm very good at secretarial work, but people have a real prejudice against employing big people like me. They immediately assume that you're lazy.

When I first went to the Victoria Hall it used to be heaving. I've watched it get emptier and emptier. My best friend, who I grew up with, still goes religiously to every show. But it's getting to her now, because she knows it's coming to the end.

Giant Haystacks: I've got a new business, a commercial collection agency, collecting bad debts from all over Manchester. It's a serious job, not baseball bats. Let's put it this way. If you were a businessman and you owed £200,000, and you had ignored all the correspondence, then I'll pay you a personal visit. This will be personally embarrassing for you. I'll come to your factory, and all the people working for you will know who I am, and some will know why I've called. You must make some sort of gesture there and then: you give me £50,000 and sign an affidavit saying you'll pay £1,000 until the debt's paid off. If you slip up one month on that affidavit, I move in there and take goods off you. I'm very diplomatic. It's always something I've been interested in.

I think wrestling will be okay. Personally I'm out now for a bit, with a bad knee. The cartilage has been troubling for a while, and I put the operation off and off, but now's the time. It won't be that long, and then I'll be back.

Everything goes through a bad patch. Who'd have thought

Lloyds would be in trouble? Who'd have thought the Iron Curtain would have come down? And wrestling's still there. It's very hard to kill an institution. It's only sleeping, and soon it will reactivate.

Jackie Pallo: Shall I tell you when the decline began? The very day I left Dale Martin. I'm being serious. Not because of me – it just happened that way. That was in 1974. Johnny Dale, the top man, came down to me about three years later and said, 'Jackie, do you realize that since you left the business it's gone down bleeding hill?'

Jackie Pallo Junior: A while ago I had the idea of making television programmes that would combine the best new blood of American and British wrestlers. So we made six hours of programmes. It was recorded at the Derngate Centre, Northampton, mostly new young bloods apart from me and Johnny Kincaid and Killer Kowalski. Dad's name sold it out – about two thousand people. I booked seventy-five wrestlers and we only needed thirty. We had forty-three turn up. Thirty-six matches in one night. Central broadcast it. It cost about £80,000, but we could only get about £15,000 back for it.

Now we've decided to get more serious, and raise substantial money for our next venture. You can't produce a Ferrari for Vauxhall money. You can paint it red, you can stick a badge on it, but it ain't a Ferrari.

Jackie Pallo: We're now going to produce wrestling shows in the halls, which we will film and then sell all over the world as a package. We're still trying to raise the bulk of the money. We need £3 million. Wrestling always did run on a shoestring, but what I'm doing is not a shoestring. I can't tell you how it will differ, but it will be totally new. We have to keep some secrets. There are a dozen men over here that we've trained.

Jackie Pallo Junior: It's like *Star Trek – The Next Generation*. But if you noticed with that movie, they still had Shatner in there. And we're still having the Pallos in with the new wrestling. It makes the link with the credibility. We've got guys here, at a gym in Canterbury, and we've got guys in America being trained. It's a bit like the launch of a new rock show with new rock stars – exactly the same thing. All the merchandise must be set up. The show will not be people hitting each other with tables and chairs, but you are going to get violence, action and a phenomenal show. You're not going to get what you get down Worthing Town Hall. It will be of the nineties. Very little from the sixties would work on television now. There are exceptions. You can still look back on the '66 World Cup, or the Ali–Henry Cooper fight, or Dad and Mick's fights and the Beatles concerts – a phenomenon, but there are very few.

Jackie Pallo: We're selling the show, not the names. In my day you had to have Mick and me on, and Les Kellett with somebody and Steve Logan with somebody. Not with this one. But our wrestlers are still brilliant. We've rejected more than we've accepted. Some wrestler called me up quite recently and said, 'I'm ready to work for you.' I said, 'Darling, while you've got a hole in your arse, I shan't use you.'

Jackie Pallo Junior: Most people cannot become wrestlers. I could get you all the outfit, get you fit, but you still wouldn't have it. You can spot a real wrestler a mile off. You can walk down the beach in Italy at four in the morning and wrestlers will recognize each other. It's an attitude, a certain arrogance, a certain 'Look at me'. The guy's spent fifteen hours in the gym, the most boring thing on the planet, pushing a lump of metal until it hurts. You can teach moves, but there has to be something there in the first place. When people audition, you can tell if they're going to be any good even before they fight.

Jackie Pallo: I can tell when a bloke puts his boots on. If you personally wanted to become a wrestler I'd give you advice straight away – stick with what you do. Do you understand what I mean? Forget it. You've got no chance. You've got more chance going out with a pick and shovel and digging the roads. I don't mean that nasty. You stick with what you know.

We're not moving with this one until everything's in place. Don't get any ideas – we're the only ones who are really trying to make it big.

Adrian Street: The last time I saw Jackie I asked him how business was, and he said, 'Luvvy, if I was an undertaker people would stop fucking dying.'

I think it's awful what's happened to the scene in England. Tony Scarlo told me that he went down to the school Jackie Pallo had and it was terrible. He said none of the guys wanted to know how to wrestle – it was all, 'Have a look at this – I can jump right off the corner post.' What the fuck's that got to do with wrestling?

The trend now is all for aerial moves and high flying out of the ring, but people are so busy working for the moves that they haven't got an ounce of personality between them. You've got to bring the audience into the ring with you. If you're not telling a story in the ring, then people aren't going to come back. Wrestling has always been about telling stories.

Brian Dixon: I got a call from the cable TV company owned by the *Mirror*, and they wanted to broadcast our shows, but there was no money involved. They wanted to do it like the old days, 4 pm on a Saturday. Also, I've heard that *Saint and Greavsie* and the *World of Sport* are coming back, although what that will entail I don't know. So there is a light there. I'd have to say that if television did come back to wrestling it would be sensational, but also the biggest headache imaginable. After WWF, and looking at the talent we've got here, it would be very difficult to see the success of it.

A few weeks ago, whoever owns the rights to the Power Rangers got their solicitors and made me sign a declaration saying that I would never use the name again.

Strangely, the solicitors were the same ones that WWF use, and the way they got hold of me was so dodgy. A woman called up saying she wanted to book a show with the Power 'Restlin' Rangers and asking all sorts of questions. I smelt a rat, and I was very dubious. She said it was for a company fête, and that she heard the Power 'Restlin' Rangers were a tremendous act. I quoted her a price, an inflated price, and she didn't bat an eyelid. She said, 'Have you got any photographs of them?' and 'Where will they be appearing next?'

They caught me out, because I got a writ for the two shows I mentioned to them, Lewisham and Croydon. So I had to give an undertaking, and change the name and the outfits. By then I had four different guys, four different coloured Rangers. So they just became the 'Restlin' Rangers, without the Power. And to be honest with you, they're losing their appeal.

Dave Soulman Bond: Things just got gradually less and less. I got disillusioned with the wrestling, because people didn't have the same sort of background. My last bout I went into the dressing room and there was no one there who had been an amateur. You know you can go in there and twist these guys inside out, these so-called showmen. I could show them. Towards the end you just didn't get the same sort of test. They did the showman bit, and that was good, or sometimes even that wasn't any good, but they couldn't wrestle. And the public began to realize.

Simon Garfield: The British Bulldog was acquitted of all charges in his pub-brawl trial. He returned to the ring in the same week as American television viewers witnessed the debut of a new heavy-weight contender, a man who called himself Loch Ness Monster. British fans would have recognized him as Giant Haystacks; his knee operation had done little to hinder his career.

Pat Roach: I've got nothing against American wrestlers, but the British boys are the best, and I think that's still probably just about true. The Spanish are always very quick, but there's not so much science. The Spanish are like comedians firing off jokes so fast you haven't got time to laugh at them. But the British would fire something off and you'd have time to absorb it.

I can remember walking into a wrestling match and there'd be silence, silent admiration, like walking into a movie theatre. You'd be just in time to see Tibby Szakacs going to his bridge and then whipping out, and there'd be a burst of applause and then quiet again waiting for his next tantalizing move. You don't often see that these days, mostly they're kicking each other in the bollocks before the bell goes.

Brian Dixon doesn't book me at all any more. At the reunion I was talking to the other guys and they all said the business was awful – I thought it was only me who wasn't doing much.

Mal Sanders: It used to be a glamour thing. We were Rock Hudsons, and there used to be beautiful women. Now we get changed in broom cupboards, with only cold water from rusting taps, one step up from a toilet attendant.

The fellows coming in now don't know a wristlock from a padlock. Everyone had a speciality in the old days. Now no one has, or they're pinching everyone else's. When you were a champion in the old days it meant something. Now? Nah. I was European Champion at twenty years old – brilliant. Now you could have five title belts, but it would mean nothing.

These days you just need the boots. Someone said it would take half a day to become a professional wrestler, but I'd say it would take at least a day. As I was saying to Lee Bronson, it's like an era in your life ending. When we started, things like *The Sweeney* were on TV, and when you see those repeats you want those great times back again. Wrestling was all we've ever known, and now it's coming to an end.

Les Kellett, Letter 6 December 1995:

Dear Simon or Mr S Garfield,

I will let you have just a few bad words first.

Although I wrestled for the promoter who started the whole cooperation off, I cannot assist you in your book.

Some of the wrestlers you spoke to must have given you stories of a rather lurid nature regarding L Kellett. In fact your research seems so thorough it makes me looking forward to it being in the shops and myself first in the queue.

Wrestlers like Mr Pat Roach came into the business at a late date, as did the officers now running the Wrestlers' Union. They assured me they had it all tied up.

Yes, I was in the old city centre one day and met a very old friend, Dennis Mitchell, one of the top heavyweights, and of course we chatted of this and that. In fact I was surprised that Dennis got a few days a week as a chauffeur.

Thank you Mr Garfield for your interest in an elderly wrestler.

L Kellett

P.S. Thank you for your monetary offer, but it – money that is – doesn't excite me anymore.

Les.

Just a few more words Simon regarding the Wrestlers' Union. I have been a member of four unions which were smashed by promoters easier than breaking a crab up with a 4 lb hammer.

Les.

Simon – I hate myself at refusing you.

Les.

Wayne Bridges: I earnt a lot of money wrestling, and I wrestled all over – Japan, US – and I made it to the very top. But I've paid the price. I was away for many months at a time, and I didn't see my son and daughter grow up, and my boy died in an accident. When you start there's no one advising you, no one to warn you how it might be. Most people weren't as ambitious as me, and they saw their family as more important, and I have to say that I think they made the right decision.

Kent Walton: Nowadays I do the occasional voice-over for commercials. Most of the film production I do is now based in South Africa, and I don't go out there much. You know Hazel Adair? She did *Crossroads* and *Emergency Ward 10*. She's my partner. She goes to South Africa and America, but it's very difficult now. We've produced about eight pictures. We did *Virgin Witch*, *Can You Keep It Up For A Week?* The one we made with EMI was something called *Keep It Up Downstairs*.

Wrestling's not the same. We need to find a lot of new young boys who want to be the new George Kidds. The showmen are not enough. The showmen are fine, but without the skill boys it doesn't work. But how do you find new fellas? They won't earn a lot of money, it can only be a sideline from other jobs, and they must really want to be thrown around, that murder of being crashed and body-slammed on the canvas, which is only a quarter of an inch thick before you get the bare boards, time and time again, night after night for years. Knowing what happened to the people who did it before them, who would want that?

I don't really go to wrestling now. It's mostly up North isn't it?

Peter Blake: I used to enjoy it enormously, in a genuine way, and I never went other than in the spirit of respect. But I don't really go any more. Clearly it's not the same, and the spirit has gone out of it. I think it's something very British we've lost, and eventually you have to accept its demise. Things have their time. I don't think you should really regret its passing. It had its day, and it was wonderful.

The rumble: 'These days you just need the boots'

Author's Note

I used to watch the wrestling on television as a small boy, fascinated and confused. What was 'real' about it didn't concern me much: I was more intrigued by the twilight arena these men inhabited, and their noisy, desperate struggle for supremacy. It seemed like a very closed world, and one I never dreamt I'd enter.

But then I met Mick McManus at his club in the Strand. Mick was a regular at the Wig and Pen, and everyone bowed as he appeared. He was wearing rep's clothes, a dark blazer and grey slacks. He was a little flabby, but retained the spring of a muzzled fighting dog. His speech was gruff and unrelenting, and he kept it low so as not to worry the other gents in the room. A club staffer hustled about, bringing tea and adjusting the heating. Mick told me why he retired. I sensed that he missed the action.

We ate side by side in the narrow downstairs restaurant, next to an old man I took to be a judge from the High Court across the road. The Wig and Pen seemed to date from medieval times, a fuggy place, dark and low. There were framed cartoons on the wall that made no sense. The club had probably never been the same since Fleet Street moved to Wapping and Canary Wharf, and since men with jobs stopped drinking at lunchtime. McManus said he tried to pop in whenever he was in town. He ordered the steak and kidney. The waiter asked whether he wanted vegetables. McManus said, 'Nah!'

I had a mushroom omelette, which I thought to be rather pricey at £8. 'That's good value that!' McManus reasoned.

Then a man called Bernard came round with the *Wig and Pen* magazine. I could join for only £150 a year, and because I was getting on so well with Mick he would waive the signing-on fee. For that there were lots of special trips to the racing and boxing.

The conversation became suddenly animated, and McManus told me about his fame and the men he used to work with, and I fancied there might be a story there.

As I went around old wrestlers' homes I toyed with the idea of becoming a wrestler myself, going a couple of bruising rounds in some deserted hall, and I tried out a few names. The Mortician. The Scribe. The Hebrew. Then I realized this would prove nothing, and would be regarded as disrespectful by the professionals who were only just beginning to treat me with something more than contempt. Also, any opponent would have hurt me very much.

Postscript

The old boys still meet at Wayne Bridges's pub, but I'm not welcome anymore. The day before I was preparing to attend the reunion in August 2006, eleven years since my first one, I received a phone call from a film director called Luke Dormehl. He was making a feature-length documentary about wrestling, and we'd been chatting about it for more than a year. But now he was calling with a warning: Wayne Bridges had taken against me. This wasn't a new thing, but a grudge held since publication of the first edition of this book.

'I was interviewing him at the pub,' Dormehl told me, 'and he said he had always been a bit suspicious of the media, but the one person he really didn't like was this person called Simon Garfinkle. I think he may have been talking about you.'

I think he probably was.

Luke went on: 'I asked him what the problem with Simon Garfinkle was, and he said it was to do with what Simon Garfinkle had written about Les Kellett.'

Oh dear. I thought I had been reasonably respectful towards Les, and had certainly given him enough of a chance to speak for himself. But now there was an added complication: Les had died. It was too late to make amends. In fact, many of the people in this book had died. Kellett, Big Daddy, Giant Haystacks, Kent Walton, Davey Boy Smith, Jackie Pallo. And 'Bomber' Pat Roach, the man who used to MC the reunions. They had – as the obituaries seldom failed to point out – all been counted out, gone to that great ring in the sky, submitted one final time. Some of their obituaries had been written by me, as I had become the go-to man for mad anecdotes. When Jackie Pallo died, Radio Four's obituary show called up, and I luxuriated once more in the Saab story.

The death of Bomber Roach affected me most, probably because he had been kindest to my book after publication (in fact, his was the only feedback I received from a wrestler). He had spoken generously of it on a television arts programme, and claimed it captured the spirit of the game. The programme had sent Roach to review a one-man play based on my book, performed with huge energy and skill by my friend Alex Lowe. Lowe played Kent Walton, Max Crabtree, Giant Haystacks, Jimmy Savile and Brian Glover, and every time I saw it I was in tears of laughter.

One person I hadn't talked to for the book, despite his appearance on the original jacket, was Kendo Nagasaki. Apparently he hadn't minded it when it was published, or at least hadn't read it, and he agreed to a meeting in 2001. This event is now a treasured memory, although at the time I was nervous of learning anything about him that would disappoint.

I was a little early for our date, which was to take place at a photographer's studio in Finsbury Park, north London. As I waited outside, I saw Nagasaki walking to the venue with his acolytes, and he wasn't yet wearing the mask. He had short brown hair, a narrow face with a prominent and slightly pinched nose, and deeply set eyes that squinted in the sunlight. He wore a dark jacket and black trousers, newly shined shoes, a nice fat metallic watch. His acolytes on this occasion consisted of his manager, his driver and his website designer. I recognised his manager first, and called out his name.

'Lloyd!'

At this moment, Kendo took his mask from his pocket. It was soft and woollen, black with white vertical stripes, and he pulled it on with some alarm. It tightened at the back with those little pop-stoppers you find on baseball caps. He suddenly looked menacing, and caused the traffic to slow.

Inside the studio, Kendo and his friends made straight for the changing room. This was one of Kendo's two stipulations: a separate changing area screened by a curtain. The second was a request for photo approval, which seemed a strange demand from a person who wears a mask. 'He's not as young as he was, and wants to make sure he looks good,' his manager explained. 'He doesn't want to blow the image at this stage.'

Picture approval was modified to a permission to view the Polaroids. He emerged from the changing area looking like a man from Japan, only taller. He had a black and gold metal visor, beneath which he had changed the black mask to red. He had a red and silver tunic, red vest and tights, high lace-up boots, a polished breastplate, and in padded gloves he held an elegant sword. In truth, it could have been anyone in there, but I knew it was Kendo because he spent the next three hours without speaking a word.

Kendo's entourage were an appealing bunch. Lawrence Stevens, a close personal assistant for a decade, was The Man Who Brings the Car Round. Wherever Kendo appears he is often pursued by people wishing to see his face, which means that the wrestler must don the black mask. But he feels awkward travelling the streets in this disguise in search of his transport, and so Lawrence always leaves a few minutes early to bring the transport as close as possible to Kendo.

Then there was Rob Cope, a long-time Kendo fan and historian, who worked at the Victoria Hall in Staffordshire, the scene of many a Nagasaki triumph. He was also helping the wrestler with his autobiography and his new Internet presence ('The Official Website of the Master of Mayhem and Mystery'). At one point during our meeting, Cope and Stevens noticed a threadbare patch on Kendo's silvery robe and tut-tutted to each other, rolling their eyes as if to say, 'That's going to cost.'

And finally there was Lloyd Ryan, Kendo's loquacious manager. He gave me a new slant on how he landed the job. One day Ryan had been watching Kendo fight in Walthamstow when he got called into the dressing room for some important news. Lawrence Stevens said: 'Look, we've got no manager, and we've decided that you are going to be the manager.' The match that evening was against 'Judo' Pete Roberts, a hard but unglamorous man from Worcester who wore red swimming trunks, and Ryan was required to hype the match before it began. 'I went in the ring and spoke a load of crap for ten minutes,' he remembered. 'The crowd started shouting and throwing things, and I thought, "Wow, I could get used to this!"'

Ryan had always seemed to me to be the obvious way to learn more about Nagasaki's real persona, and so a few weeks before the photo session we struck a deal. He said that Kendo would agree to be interviewed, but only in writing. I would prepare some questions, Ryan would fax them to Kendo's lair somewhere in the Potteries, and the scales would fall from our eyes. The simplest of plans.

The answers came back not by fax but in blue flowery biro. 'Do you have a family?' I asked Nagasaki. 'Any hobbies?'

'None that I am in regular contact with,' he replied. 'Hobbies: boating, horse riding.' (He also wrote 'I own a boat . . . ' but then scribbled it out.)

Q: How do you spend your time these days?

A: I divide my time between business activities and leisure pursuits. I am a director of several companies, but do not take part in the day-to-day running.

Q: How would you describe the state of wrestling in the UK today?

A: UK wrestling no longer exists. It's an abortion of Americanized entertainment. There is no longer any originality – the business does not attract the characters it once did.'

Q: Is there any way back for it?

A: No way back at all. The scene had become stale long before Greg Dyke took it off. The nail in the coffin was the introduction of the US tapes. The whole of the business there is based on comic-book creations, everyone has to appear superhuman. The persona of Nagasaki was always greatly theatrical and as such wouldn't be out of place in the American market, but he is the exception over here.

Q: Can you explain the significance of the salt and the red and black masks?

A: The idea of the salt is a cleansing process, to cleanse the spirit through the contest so that no animosity is felt afterwards. The black mask has become a symbol of meditation for me. I only don the red mask shortly before I enter the ring – it means that Kendo is fully manifested within me.

Q: Your wrestling persona is brutal and unforgiving. Are these traits purely confined to the ring?

A: Kendo's aggression is saved entirely for the ring. There is a period of wind-down following a match when the aggressive nature of Nagasaki is shed and a more harmonious persona is regained.

Q: Inside the ring I do not remember any displays of humour . . .

A: The humour was always in George ['Gorgeous' George Gillette, previous manager], not in Nagasaki, although it is fair to say that he made me laugh on occasions at his antics. I do enjoy true-to-life humour. I don't find comedians funny, but something like Willy Russell's *Blood Brothers*, despite being ultimately a tragedy, contains the sort of earthy humour that I personally find very funny.

Q: Do you regret the unmasking?

A: I do not regret it, the reaction was very surprising. For many years there had been hatred towards Nagasaki, yet when the mask came off the audience gave me a genuine standing ovation which was quite thrilling.

Q: Would it be fair to say that Kendo Nagasaki's ring persona is in some way compensating for an unhappy childhood?

A: Yes. My childhood created the need to explore an alternative identity.

Q: How did you lose part of your finger?

A: I offer no explanations or claims, despite various inaccurate explanations offered by some people . . .

In 1990 Nagasaki appeared on a discussion programme on Granada television in which various wrestlers campaigned for a right to have their matches televised again. Inevitably, Kendo just sat there without saying anything, but at the very end of the show he became annoyed with one of the other wrestlers and began throwing him around. This was a prearranged scuffle, but it was news to a female make-up artist standing nearby. This woman, who had been Sir Laurence Olivier's personal make-up artist for several years, hit her head against the wall, was briefly unconscious, and woke up in terrible pain. The accident ended her career.

Shortly afterwards, the broadcasting workers' union BECTU decided to sue Granada and Nagasaki on her behalf. The case lasted seven years. Granada attempted to shift all responsibility towards Nagasaki, who was not insured. But the judge ruled that Nagasaki had only been doing what he was told, and ordered Granada to pay the make-up artist compensation of £327,000 plus costs.

Q: What can you tell me about your involvement with the healing arts?

A: I very seldom practice my healing techniques these days. For a time, my work in this field was very successful. I don't these days have a healing clinic, although I'm pleased to say there is a long list of people who have testified to my abilities in this area.

Q: How would you sum up your experience of managing rock bands? [In the eighties, Nagasaki and Gillette guided the career of the Cuddly Toys, among others.]

A: Rock is a very cut-throat industry, but I had a lot of fun. Had it not been for George's illness, I would probably have stayed in the field a little longer.

Q: What are your thoughts on the euro?

A: Entry into the European Community does generally seem to me to be a good idea, so I would support adoption of the euro. I would like Kenneth Clarke as the next leader of the Conservative Party.

Q: How would you like to be remembered?

A: As British wrestling's greatest masked wrestler. Having been voted Wrestler of the Millennium by the fans recently it would seem I have achieved that goal. Peter Blake's portrait has also added to a certain immortality.

*

Kendo is now retired, but when I met him Peter Blake was helping out at his final appearances in the ring.

'A few months ago I agreed to appear with him at a charity show he was doing for the mentally handicapped,' Blake told me. 'I was introduced in the normal way – you know, the man who did the Sgt Pepper album – and the person who presented me was very impressed that I'd got a CBE. Then there was the normal shenanigans with Lloyd Ryan. He said to me, "Call yourself a painter? I wouldn't let you paint my bathroom." It was a lot of fun.'

The friends met up again at the opening of a new exhibition at Agnew's art gallery in Old Bond Street. A young artist called Peter Lloyd had made a series of prints about masked Mexican wrestlers, and Nagasaki and Blake found them hard to resist. Over drinks and nibbles, Mark Adams, Agnew's director of contemporary art, introduced Kendo as the guest of honour, and the wrestler stood around in full visor and cape looking serene. The partygoers were blasé, as if Nagasaki was just the latest type of stripogram.

'Kendo got a bang on the head last week because someone ran into the back of his boat,' Peter Blake told me. 'So now his jaw is all hurt and he can hardly talk even if he wants to.' Blake calls Kendo 'Peter' when he doesn't have the mask on, but never when he's in character. 'He needs a good period of silent meditation to become Kendo. It's not like a light bulb you can just switch on and off. He treats Kendo as a separate entity and talks of him sometimes in the third person.'

As we were talking, Kendo decided it was time to leave. He left the gallery looking smart but casual, and waited for Lawrence to bring the car round, a bottle-green Rover Vitesse. Nagasaki manoeuvred himself into the passenger seat and they headed down Old Bond Street, left into Piccadilly, and it was not until they had passed the Royal Academy that Kendo decided it was safe to remove the disguise. They were on their way to the boat in Brighton for a spot of fairweather sailing.

Kendo didn't turn up to the 2006 reunion, and nor did I. There was just too much heat on me. I heard that it was still a great event, though not without its misfortunes. For a start, not everyone could make it. According to a report on the reunion website ('Strengthening the Ring of Friendship'), Mick McManus wasn't there because someone in his family was poorly, and others had sent similar apologies and complex reasons: 'Bad' Bobby Barnes was recovering from knee surgery at his villa in Bulgaria (there's a whole book in that sentence); Ray Fury was recovering from the death of his wife in Turkey; Johnny Czeslaw was also mourning the death of his wife; Bazal Riley now lived in Tenerife; Johnny Elijah, Spencer Churchill and Joe 'Dazzler' Cornelius were all sick. The good news was that Mark 'Rollerball' Rocco had managed to make it over from the sunny Med, as had Jim 'Cry Baby' Breaks, who lived in Gran Canaria. I was sad to miss the appearance of Paul Lincoln, who had found masked fame as Dr Death, especially as I had recently met his son Aaron Lincoln, who was now managing England football captain John Terry.

The catering was handled by Wayne Bridges's wife Sarah, a champion bodybuilder. She had bought more than £500-worth of ingredients, but not enough care had been taken with security. Accordingly, some people began throwing sausage rolls. Also, the splendid cake that had been made for the event, in the shape of a wrestling ring, was completely forgotten about, and had to be given away shortly afterwards to an old-age home.

There were many young people in attendance at the reunion, some of them teenage wrestlers, and it was apparent that the British wrestling scene was undergoing something of a resurgence. Klondyke Kate and Robbie Brookside still pounded the boards, and they were joined by kids who used to watch them twenty years before. Much of their ringside training involved the smashing of chairs and other props – the American influence. But they were keen to entertain, and were brave. They were spurred on, perhaps, by the nostalgic regular sequence on Sky's *Soccer AM*, which had repopularized the Big Daddy chant of 'Easy! Easy!' by putting it in the mouth of a thin guy dressed as Kendo.

The wrestling scene in the United States has changed significantly since this book was first published. The World Wrestling Federation (WWF) is now World Wrestling Entertainment (WWE) following a copyright suit in 2000 from the World Wildlife Fund. Some of the old guard still pump themselves up for combat on Monday night television, where they are joined by the likes of Rey Mysterio and Mickie James (a woman), but the scene is clearly not what it was during its heyday in the mid-1990s. Davey Boy Smith died of a heart attack in 2002, his coroner citing anabolic steroids as a possible contributory factor.

Many of the ITV *World of Sport* bouts that were missing-pre-sumed-wiped have turned up. Some of these form the basis of the *Best of ITV Wrestling*, a recent DVD in which one has the unusu-al opportunity to watch Giant Haystacks gain nine stone in the course of an hour. During his first outing on this compilation he is partnering Big Daddy in a tag-team contest from 1975, and a short while later he is fighting against Daddy at Wembley Arena in 1981. In the interim he has gone from 31 stone to 40 stone, and the technical side of his game has suffered, giving way to the barging-and-shoving side. In their final bout, Haystacks and Daddy bellyflop each other for three minutes until Haystacks falls through the ropes onto a nice ringside flower arrangement and is counted out. 'Easy! Easy!' can be heard when Daddy (who has 'Sock It To 'Em' sewn onto the seat of his pants) is joined in the ring by two very young majorettes.

Watching Catweazle, Vic Faulkner, Bomber Roach and Rollerball Rocco on these tapes, I was reminded how significant had been the role of the referee in these bouts. Apart from Max Ward, who looked like Arthur Mullard, they tended to be tiny squits who were invariably hit 'by accident' when a wrestler ducked, and riled the crowd by missing some skulduggery inflicted while looking the wrong way.

The DVD is introduced by Dickie Davies in silver hair and bronze tan, who asserts that wrestling 'was water-cooler TV before they invented water coolers'. In the eighties, before they invented revisionism, I remember Davies judging the wrestling less favourably because it wasn't a real sport.

In February 2006 I shared a cup of tea with Davies in a photo-graphic studio in Clerkenwell. I was writing a story about old sports commentators and presenters, and over the radio came the news of the death of Jackie Pallo. 'It's the only time he's not faking it,' Davies said. Talking to him made me realize again how much I missed those old guys. They had a spectacular talent, and it was a joy and privilege to have met them.

Acknowledgements

I would like to thank everyone who helped me with this book, particularly those who agreed to be interviewed. As may be apparent from the text, Mick McManus, Joe D'Orazio, Max Crabtree, Brian Dixon and Robbie Brookside proved especially generous with their time, and I am extremely grateful. I would also like to thank Richard Dennis, Derek Ridgers, Geoff Woad, David Annen and Kipper Williams.

Along with his letter, Les Kellett sent me two unused first-class postage stamps – recompense, I imagine, for not replying to my earlier requests for an interview. Initially I was disappointed with his refusal, but it didn't take long to convince myself it was for the best. Perhaps some memories should be left alone, forever at their hardest, complete only in other minds.

The majority of the interviews for this book were conducted in 1995. Some took place in 1992, for a piece in the *Independent on Sunday Review*, a few in 1996. I have also quoted from the following: Charles B Cochran, *Showman Looks On* (J. M. Dent & Sons, 1945); Kent Walton, *This Grappling Game* (Neville Spearman, 1967); Sir Atholl Oakeley, *Blue Blood on the Mat* (Stanley Paul, 1971); Roland Barthes, *Mythologies* (Jonathan Cape, 1972); Richard Crossman, *The Diaries of a Cabinet Minister* (Hamish Hamilton & Jonathan Cape, 1977); Jackie Pallo, *You Grunt, I'll Groan* (Queen Anne Press, 1985).

Pictures: pp. x, 78, 93, 175, 178–9, 197, 198, 200, 212 by Derek Ridgers; line drawings p. 8 from *Showman Looks On*, B. Cochran; p. 70 by Dennis Hutchinson, *Sunday People*; p. 75 from *TV Times*; pp. 87, 89, 97 from *You Grunt, I'll Groan*, Jackie Pallo; p. 119 copyright the *Guardian*; p. 129 by Mary Dickinson.

Index

Kendo–Haystacks match referee,
135; at end of televised
wrestling, 144–5; not doing
much now, 208

Roberts, Peter, 131; injures
Masambula, 95–6

Robin, Andy, 49

Robin Hood, Prince of Thieves, 103

Rocco, Mark Rollerball, 59, 131,
187

Rogers, Buddy, 73

Rolling Stones, 61, 66

Rome, 35

Ross, Edmundo, 126

Royal, Bert, 25

Royal Albert Hall *see* Albert Hall

Royal Brothers, 109

Royal College of Art, 120

royal family: as wrestling fans,
55–6, 59–60, 114, 144, 150;
included a masked professional
wrestler, 122

Royal Shakespeare Company, 35–6

rules of wrestling, 17–18, 20, 21

Russian Lion (Georges
Hackenschmidt), 14–17

Ryan, Lloyd: on Dr Death, 123; and
Kendo Nagasaki, 123, 124–5,
126, 129–31, 135, 136; and
music business, 126; does some
wrestling, 131

Saffron Walden, 122

Saint, Johnny, 187

St Clair, Tony, 95, 187

St George's Hall, Liverpool, 192–4,
195

Saint and Greavsie, 207

Salford: Royal Infirmary, 52

Samoa, Western, 140

Sanders, Mal: on modern technology, 77; and Mike Marino, 79,
80–1, 83–4; wrestling career, 79,
80, 83, 84, 154; on choreography
of wrestling, 94–5; on Dr Death,
122; as Big Daddy's tag partner,

154; 'we were Rock Hudsons',
208–9

Savage, Lily, 116

Savalas, Telly, 60

Savile, Jimmy: as wrestler, 52–3

Scala, Bob *see* D'Orazio, Joe

Scarlo, Tony, 207

Schumann, Franz, 138–9

Scotland, 25, 49; Edinburgh, 19,
127; King George Hall, Glasgow,
26; Aberdeen, 111

Scott, Charlie Big Boy, 31

Second World War, 20, 21

Shakespeare, William: *As You Like
It*, 35–6

Shatner, William, 205

Shaw, George Bernard: meets
Georges Hackenschmidt, 17

Sheffield, 19

Shelton, Bill, 30–1

Shephard, Wildon, 34

Shinfield, Billy, 96

showbusiness, 89–90, 91, 92–3,
94–5; in America, 163, 166; the
Power Ranger, 179, 186, 193; the
Bushwhackers, 193, 194, *see also*
World Wrestling Federation
(WWF)

Shrewsbury, 97

Shuds, Dave 'Slappy', 179

Shyster, Tax Inspector Irwin R., 160

Sid Millwall's Nitwits, 50–1

Sinatra, Frank: co-manages Sky
High Lee, 51; meets 'Mr
Haystacks', 60

Singh, Tiger Kashmir, 178, 181,
197, 198

Skinner, Mr Justice, 96

Sky Lo Lo, 122

Sky television, 146, 158

Slynn, Mr Justice, 113–14

Smith, Davey Boy (the British
Bulldog), 160, 168, 169, 170–4;
charged with assault, 173; acquitted, 208

Smith, Harvey: as wrestler, 53